The
Symbolist Movement

D0082613

The
Symbolist Movement

⊚⊚⊚

A CRITICAL APPRAISAL
by
Anna Balakian
NEW YORK UNIVERSITY

New York • New York University Press • 1977

Library of Congress Catalog Card Number: 77-76044

ISBN: 0-8147-0993-1 cloth
0-8147-0994-x pbk

Manufactured in the United States of America

To my husband, Stepan Nalbantian

PREFACE

This book is intended as a critical appraisal of the Symbolist Movement from its origins in French literature to the literary conventions it created in the European literature of the end of the nineteenth and early twentieth centuries. It is offered as a succinct synthesis to serve as a guide to the study of symbolism from the point of view of comparative literature. It is perforce eclectic in approach; its only historical feature will lie in the observance of chronology in the organization of the chapters. In view of the large maze of writing grouped under the flexible label of "symbolism," a definition is not possible; through this focusing, however, it is hoped that the reader may gain a composite image, based on the salient qualities which have been associated with the movement. In this spirit, I offer what follows as one more step in the long process of sifting the wheat from the chaff, as we gain distance from the source. The bibliography will help fill the gaps. Poetry quoted in languages not readily accessible has been largely paraphrased, or its importance as illustrative material explained sufficiently to overcome the necessity for translation. All of the translations, except where otherwise noted, are mine.

I deeply appreciate New York University's liberal policy of a year's sabbatical leave without which the writing of this book would have been impossible. A further grant from the Graduate School's research fund accelerated the preparation of the manuscript. My thanks to Stephanie Hawthorne and Mary Ann Amdur of the Romance Language Department for their aid in typing and checking data, and to my many students in Comparative Literature whose explorations of literatures foreign to me brought fresh light on the common heritage of symbolism. I am grateful for my sister Nona's editorial suggestions and for the infinite pains and precisions of Nina Blaustein of Random House in the preparation of the manuscript for publication. My deep appreciation to my husband and children for their understanding and patience as I took away time—but not love—from them to do this study.

Finally, I thank my friend Professor Haskell Block, who made the original suggestion to me to write this book, which is the product of a class on Symbolism in the Comparative Literature Division of New York University. It came out of a classroom, and it is returned to the classroom for what aid it may give to others in the pursuit of literary forms that cut across national frontiers.

A.B.

INTRODUCTION TO 1977 EDITION

Ten years have passed since the first printing of this small book on the Symbolist Movement. Those who expressed astonishment at the time that a two hundred page study dared cover a literary movement of such magnitude overlooked the second part of my title: "a critical appraisal." I was not attempting to compete either with Guy Michaud nor Kenneth Cornell, the two prestigious historians of the Symbolist Movement which affected poetic *écriture* and philosophical attitudes for a longer period of time than did Romanticism, and which encompassed literature more globally than any previous movement.

I thought that the time had come to peruse its topography from temporal distances and to discern towering figures (what Apollinaire called "collines") and unifying features. With the passage of nearly a century since Rimbaud discovered that "so many egotists think themselves poets," and of a good half-century since the movement's presumed waning, I deemed that Symbolism was ready for critical discrimination and unconventional judgements; it was time for deserved remembrances and kind forgetfulnesses, for highlights and omissions, and particularly for neglect and disregard of the self-serving and unapplied theories of its activists which needs must crowd the pages of Histories of Symbolism. In retrospect, what I had realized in fact was that the best of symbolist poetry actually emerged before and after the period of the cénacle, that the fruit of Symbolism was more glorious than its flowering. When the prolific *Symbolistes* are reduced to representative roles it becomes clearer to discern the total curve of the literary movement they named and which was to become one of the richest veins of modern poetry.

If the first result of my critical study was to realize the need to readjust the focus of symbolism, the next was to observe the avatars evident far into the twentieth century. Since the publication of this book I have had the opportunity to observe many more of these transformations of the original Symbolist School, and were I to rewrite this book today, it would indeed be longer and reach farther into modern literature. As it is, I am suggesting the extensions of the frontiers of symbolism in an afterword where I consider the wider interpretations and recognitions of symbolist *écriture*.

Leaving appraisal aside, it must be heralded here that the very History of Symbolism is currently undergoing modifications: a massive collaborative effort on the part of some fifty-five literary historians from various countries has produced an extensive study of Symbolism soon to appear in the series of the *Comparative History of Literature in European Languages,* now in progress under the auspices of the International Comparative Literature Association. In putting this study together as its editor, I have been able to extend vastly my own knowledge of unfamiliar literatures that were so deeply involved in shaping and nourishing the international symbolist movement, sometimes under alternate labels such as aestheticism, hermeticism, modernismo. The variations suggested by these titles, just as elusive as the original one of "symbolism," shared an inherent doctrine and contributed to a plethora of poetry. Symbolism created a kinship among poets wherever poetry has been written in the past century.

The concept of "influence" is often viewed as an imperialistic invasion, and given a pejorative meaning. No one is willing to admit to being influenced, and everyone is loath to study influence simply because of its unfortunate association and confusion with the word *imitation*. For too long the influence of Symbolism has been considered a process leading to the discovery of an inferior brand of French Symbolism in other European countries. The truth that comes to light when the salient features of symbolist aesthetics are studied globally is that French Symbolism served as a potent catalyst for other national literatures but underwent mutations and transformations under the forces of local myths and stylistic conventions. In fact the symbolist factor becomes indispensable to the understanding of poetic developments in virtually every national literature of the period. Poetry through the language of symbolism created a delicate ontology uniting poets across frontiers; they sang not in unison but in keys that concorded and produced a magnificent harmony across the universe, untouched by rampant wars and political disruptions. I have also come to recognize that what we tend to call "minor" literatures are often literatures that are simply unfamiliar to the Western European and American readership for which critical writings on Comparative Literature are generally destined. We shall have to work harder to bring the gems of these unfamiliar literatures into the mainstream of our critical frame of reference. Their place in the total history of the Symbolist Movement is integral and must become recognized.

If the national literatures represented in this study seem minimal in my wider knowledge of the extent of the symbolist imprint, the bibliography herewith included obviously also needs enlarging. But in the interim we have done some teamwork in this respect as well. With generous assistance from the National

Endowment for the Humanities, a monumental bibliographical work has resulted, initiated under my direction, researched by two National Endowment fellows, Diane Savoye and Georgia Maas, completed and professionally classified by Professor David Anderson. It was published by New York University Press in 1975 and is comprehensive on an international scale to 1974. It should prove a useful tool for researchers in the field. It will suffice, therefore, for me to mention here just a few noteworthy contributions to our understanding of the Symbolist Movement which have appeared since the earlier printing of my book. They are Manfred Gsteiger's *Französische Symbolisten in der deutschen Literatur der Jahrhundetwende,* André Karatson's *Le Symbolisme en Hongrie,* Henri Peyre's *Qu'est-ce que le Symbolisme,* James Lawler's *The Language of French Symbolism.* James Kugel's *The Techniques of Strangeness in Symbolist Poetry,* James Boon's *From Symbolism to Structuralism,* J. M. Aguirre's *Antonio Machado, poeta simbolista,* and Michel Benamou's extraordinary book, *L'Oeuvre-Monde de Wallace Stevens,* which illuminates the symbolist character of Stevens' poetry precisely and extensively.

There is another aspect of the symbolist impact to be noted here, and which will no doubt draw more attention in years to come. When symbolism is viewed in terms of its central visionary quality rather than in its specifically recognizable conventions, the role of myth at the center of its aesthetics and of its analogical patterns makes us more sensitive to the freer involvement of authors heretofore not drawn into its context by literary historians: symbolists without conscious indoctrination, writers without a party membership, whose assimilation of symbolist sensitivity was a veritable symbiosis, inherent in their expression of orphic descents and angelic ascensions, of veils created and lifted, of oracular use of language and silences communicated, cognizant of that larger reality, sensed by Balzac when he defined the realists as a "family of restless dreamers, seekers of the unexpected." In that larger context writers such as Samuel Beckett, Anais Nin, Emilio Montale, Henry Miller, George Seferis can be seen to appertain to the symbolist heritage. Demonstrative of these unexpected symbolist gleanings is a perceptive work by Professor Bertrand Mathieu on Henry Miller, called *Orpheus in Brooklyn,* in which the author accomplishes the remarkable feat of demonstrating the symbolist qualities of a writer heretofore mostly associated with the seamier side of realism. This aspect of Miller's work becomes impressively recognizable as the illuminatory voyance of Rimbaud floods Miller's *Colossus of Maroussi.*

As we approach this century's "decadent" period, the study of the nineteenth-century symbolist heritage helps us to distinguish between the overt denunciations of human failures which are part of the cultural inventory of our time, and that other expression of a failing more intrinsically part of the human condition: the fatal flaw of the rose. In an age when the notion of beauty is virtually dead, the symbolist sanctum offers a refuge not unlike Herodiade's chamber. Anais Nin's "cities of the interior" are the last settings of that rare aesthetic experience echoed from decade to decade in a universal language unique in its power to be at once hermetic and communicative.

The Symbolist cénacle's most significant achievement perhaps was to initiate the priesthood of the poet for these irreligious times, endowing it with a ritual and language of its own.

In the end was the Word. . . .

CONTENTS

The
Symbolist Movement

INTRODUCTION: THE MEANING OF THE WORD

Although elusive in meaning, the term "symbolism" has become a convenient label for literary historians to designate the post-Romantic era. At the same time, it has provided a target for those literary critics who consider symbolism an artificial classification of heterogeneous writers, separated from each other in terms of nationality, time, and literary genre.

To the French, "Symbolism" still denotes technically the period between 1885 and 1895, during which it became a widely espoused literary movement and as a *cénacle* produced manifestoes, sponsored literary periodicals such as *La Revue Wagnérienne, La Vogue, Revue Indépendante,* and *La Décadence,* and attracted to Paris poets and literary personalities from all parts of the Western world. As a specific literary school, "symbolism" may best be written with a capital "S."

Critics in the Anglo-Saxon world, on the other hand, taking their cue from Arthur Symons, who was a contemporary of Verlaine and Rimbaud, tend to think of French "symbolism" (this time it is best written with a small "s") in terms of the "big four" of French poetry of the second half of the nineteenth century: Baudelaire, Rimbaud, Verlaine, Mallarmé. Using the word "symbolism" in the same broad sense as Symons,

T. S. Eliot added to the list such noncoterie poets as
Laforgue and Corbière. C. M. Bowra, in his introduction to *The Heritage of Symbolism,* links Baudelaire,
Verlaine, and Mallarmé as the avant-garde of the symbolist movement on the basis of their great innovations
in terms of literary techniques. In this way, Bowra encompasses within the symbolist tradition all those poets
who "attempted to convey a supernatural experience in
the language of visible things, and therefore almost
every word is a symbol and is used not for its common
purpose but for the association which it evokes of a
reality beyond the senses." [1] He calls these poets "post-
symbolists," as does Kenneth Cornell in his book *The
Post-Symbolist Period.* The prefix "post," however, implies a greater separation from the symbolist tradition
than there really was. This flexible use of the term em-
braces writers, posterior to the Symbolist generation,
who accepted the Symbolist school and who, through
their total or partial adherence to its poetic principles
or mystical orientation, maintained the presence of symbolism as a literary convention and signature well into
the twentieth century. The fact is that the heirs of Symbolism are today more prominent in the annals of
literary history than those who founded the Symbolist
school. Such diversified works as those of Valéry, Rilke,
Hofmannsthal, Yeats, Jiménez, Wallace Stevens, A. A.
Blok, and to some extent T. S. Eliot have shared the
legacy.[2]

The literary critics and historians of symbolism have
been almost as numerous and as nationally diverse as
the adherents themselves. Sometimes their studies have
mirrored the critic's own spiritual image; sometimes
they have been documentary records of the events that

[1] C. M. Bowra, *The Heritage of Symbolism* (London: Macmillan, 1943), p. 5.

[2] In appraising the symbolist aesthetics, the distinction between the original *cénacle* and the evolution of the movement
during the late nineteenth and twentieth centuries may help
to clarify the literary fortune of its basic characteristics.

marked the concerted activities of the Symbolist writers. Others have scanned the far reaches in space and time of what was one of the closest intellectual alliances in European history, marked by a cosmopolitanism totally devoid of self-consciousness or political intent. Still others have traced the sources of symbolism back to the literary traditions of the common European heritage.[3] There is not much left to be added to all these works.[4]

From the beginning, the hybrid movement has presented a difficult research problem—the classification of writings, profuse and seemingly disparate in form and intent, held together by a label which had from the very start multiple connotations. The earliest studies, such as André Barre's *Le Symbolisme: essai historique,* classified the symbolists in tight, genealogical categories on the basis of generations, and without any attempt to distinguish major from minor poets. In fact, some of those whom time and distance have reduced to minor status were so voluble during their lifetime that they loomed great to their contemporaries and distorted critical judgment.

In opposition to this chronological classification, there has developed a tendency to demonstrate that the relationship among many of these poets was a common negative reaction to existing literary traditions which stemmed from Romantic conventions. In his study *The Symbolist Movement,*[5] Kenneth Cornell describes this attitude: "The resolve not to accept a pattern was stronger than the desire to create a formula." This attitude, which indicates a common

[3] A provocative book by Angelo P. Bertocci traces the background of symbolism, in its broad sense, back to Plotinus. In that perspective Baudelaire becomes a summit of symbolism rather than a threshold. Hence the title *From Symbolism to Baudelaire* (Carbondale: Southern Illinois Press, 1964).

[4] For a review of recent studies see A. Balakian, "Studies in French Symbolism, 1945–1955," *The Romanic Review,* XLVI, 3 (October 1955), 223–30.

[5] Kenneth Cornell, *The Symbolist Movement* (New Haven: Yale University Press, 1951).

climate rather than a common aesthetics, has tended
to show how artificial was the original hierarchy, based
more or less on the self-evaluation of the theorists
among the Symbolists. The most famous book on symbolism viewed as a spiritual alliance is Edmund Wilson's *Axel's Castle*. Wilson identified the symbolist
image with the recluse hero of Villiers de l'Isle-Adam's
poetic drama *Axël* which, unread and unperformed,
has left an indelible mark as the symbol of the in-
habitant of our latter-day ivory towers of inner existence. Defining the symbolist mode of writing in terms
of this withdrawal into private worlds of thought and
cryptic styles of communication, Wilson was able to
include in the orbit of symbolism such widely varying
writers as T. S. Eliot, Proust, Gertrude Stein, and the
Dadaists.

Rejection of the world and revolt against the accepted ways of writing have been the theme and variations of studies on symbolism by Paul Valéry, Guy
Michaud, and Albert Thibaudet, to mention but a
few. Another line of symbolist studies has concentrated
on the psychological traumas of the symbolist cult.
Such a work is Svend Johansen's *Le Symbolisme*,[6]
which gives a detailed account of the techniques' of
synesthesia. Still another group of critics have studied
symbolism from the point of view of the differences
rather than the affinities discernible among the so-
called symbolists. When Léon Guichard evaluates
Laforgue [7] and Jacques Gengoux appraises Mallarmé [8]
it is primarily in order to show how non-symbolist
these symbolists really were. According to such studies
symbolism might be considered a superficial cloak to

[6] Svend Johansen, *Le Symbolisme* (Copenhagen: Einar Munksgaard, 1945).

[7] Léon Guichard, *Jules Laforgue et ses poésies* (Paris: Presses
Universitaires de France, 1950).

[8] Jacques Gengoux, *Le Symbolisme de Mallarmé* (Paris: Nizet,
1950).

hide realism, classicism, or simply another phase of the Parnassian ideal. Works such as these make one wonder if the word "symbolism" was indeed a face without features, an expression tossed about for the purpose of mystification. If it had no common denominator, then its validity as a critical term would be questionable. To be negotiable in critical exchange, a literary label must have either temporal significance or qualitative content. Since works dating anywhere from 1857 (the year Baudelaire's *Les Fleurs du Mal* was published) to the 1930's can be termed "symbolist," the time element is invalid. The problem that faces us then is whether the techniques of symbolism are equally unreliable when taken as yardsticks of literary values. Judging from recent criticism such as that cited above, it could be assumed that the qualitative element might also be discounted. One begins to wonder then to what extent "symbolism" may entirely be disqualified as a literary label!

Before we banish the term, however, we must remember that the disagreements as to its meaning are not limited to the fate of the word "symbolism" but rather are indicative of a general tendency in criticism to debunk all labels. So much, for instance, of what used to be called "classical" is now just "baroque." In reaction against previously tight classifications, there is a tendency today to disengage what is non-classical in a classicist, non-romantic in a romanticist, and—more pertinent to our subject—what is non-symbolist in a symbolist. But in this general desire to free the individuality of authors from group commitments, it is well to remember that, however arbitrary classifications may seem, they are necessary safeguards against the vagaries of impressionistic criticism and biographical digressions. If, as some believe, there is a loss of the particular identity of the author through categorization by labels, it is equally dangerous to leave him in a

vacuum and to attribute solely to his personal assets
or faults those traits that are in truth the stylization of
a common heritage.

Negative values would not have sufficed to produce
an affiliation among a galaxy of poets; the fact that
symbolism proved powerful enough to cross national,
linguistic, and geographical barriers provides strong
evidence that there existed a single fountainhead, and
a primary derivative. If the name has survived while
many of those who bore it have fallen into oblivion,
this was more than a marriage of convenience. Many of
the seeming disparities were often nothing more than
a series of partial defaults or deviations from a chosen
ideal and philosophy of writing. The clarification of
some of the ambiguities of the *ars poetica* of symbolism may bring into better focus the broad base of unity
that is inherent among those writers who shared in the
symbolist ideal in the course of several generations.

To construct a composite definition of symbolism
out of the miscellaneous impressions and generalizations that are associated with the word, the term must
be confronted with other literary labels of the period.
Was symbolism a reaction against Romanticism or a
continuation of its aesthetics? Was it a parallel movement to naturalism or its antithesis? What were its
tangents with such associated notions as decadent, im-
pressionist, hermetic, and imagist? To what extent did
it possess common sources with surrealism? How and
where did it best maintain its resilience against other
literary movements? What was to be symbolism's contribution to modernism? All these questions are pertinent and necessary to the study of symbolism, whose
range and variations of form have become almost as
broad as those of Romanticism.

Definition cannot be achieved without a clarification
of the ambiguities. For a term that has come to mean
so many things to so many people, misconceptions and
equivocations could not have been avoided. I shall

examine and challenge three of these: verbal mystification, the analogy between poetry and music, and the familiar antithesis implied by the early critics and poets of the symbolist movement in the expression "symbolist and decadent."

The point of departure of this study will be Symbolism as it germinated in France in the latter part of the nineteenth century and reached its greatest degree of polemic activity in the decade between 1885 and 1895. The major significance of the Symbolist school in relation to the study of symbolism in its vaster context is that it created a particular climate in which those poets and critics of England,[9] Germany, Italy, Spain, and the United States who first shared the experiences and memories of the *cénacle* convened with French writers and then took back with them their own evolved versions of the attitudes and conventions developed in Paris. Actually, much of what was to be known as symbolism abroad was based not on French Symbolism but on a translation or interpretation of French Symbolism that was in fact a mutation of the original. The degree of originality and deviation can be grasped only in relation to the full texture of the original and its intention.

Mallarmé, in whom there has since been discovered much more than symbolism, was nonetheless the uncontested poet image of Symbolism. In fact, some will insist that he is the sole poet who has survived the *cénacle*. There were those who expressed their theories in a more technical fashion, but Mallarmé acted the role of the secular priest and verbal mystifier, vividly representing thereby the two arms of the symbolist scale. Symbolism was not French; it happened in Paris. Symbolism was to be a *Parisian* movement (in distinction from *French*), Parisian in terms of its cosmopolitan character, preparing that particular interna-

9 Cf. Ruth Z. Temple, *The Critic's Alchemy* (New York: Twayne Publishers, 1853).

tional climate which has proved so propitious for
subsequent avant-garde coteries: cubism, futurism,
dadaism, and surrealism. With symbolism, art ceased
in truth to be national and assumed the collective
premises of Western culture. Its overwhelming concern
was the non-temporal, non-sectarian, non-geographic,
and non-national problem of the human condition:
the confrontation between human mortality and the
power of survival through the preservation of the
human sensitivities in the art forms.

Romanticism had been international in quite another sense; it was a contagion that attacked each
European country at its own literary hearth, as its
authors fulfilled the *mal du siècle* in a great surge of
lyricism adapted to their particular national character
and local color. Surely there is no mistaking a Novalis
for a Coleridge or a Musset. But in the Paris of the
1890's poets lost their national identity, at least temporarily, in the esoteric attitude of art; they rejected
society and, far from becoming the official voices of
their countries, they moved in closed circles communicating solely with their own breed. In the aftermath of
the political defeat of 1870, it was not the French re-
public that gave impetus to this strange communion
through which France gained artistic prestige as she
lost political power; it was rather that the French
language—thanks to its ability to be at the same time
clear and elliptical, simple and sophisticated, pure and
intricate—became the universal language of poetic
interchange. The artistic vision, freed from national
ideals, focused on the relationship between the subjective, purely personal world of the artist, and its
objective projection.

They all came to Paris: Arthur Symons, Yeats, and
George Moore from England; Stefan George, Hofmannsthal, Rilke, and Hauptmann from the German-
speaking world; Azorín and the Machado brothers
from Spain; D'Annunzio from Italy; Maeterlinck and

Verhaeren from Belgium; Moréas from Greece; Viélé-Griffin and Stuart Merrill from the United States. Paris served as the neutralizer of diverse cultural formations, and at the same time was the fertile ground on which a philosophy of art, mutually acceptable, yet subject to individual variations, could be sown.

The present study seeks no new arteries nor is its aim to uncover new mansions in the symbolist domain. It is an effort at the appraisal and definition of terms as they pertain to the study of comparative literature. In probing into the resources of symbolism, I want to be able to focus on those traits which, over and above literary theory and techniques, have left a composite family image, persistent and self-perpetuating. And, as we gain distance from the source, we can better assume the merciless task of sifting the enormous miscellany of associated writings the better to discern the summits of the terrain.

The Symbolists and their international coterie agreed on accepting a common origin in the philosophy of Swedenborg, which had already succeeded in infiltrating the art forms through such literary illuminists as Gerard de Nerval, Novalis, Blake, and Emerson. The manner of transmission had been multiple and simultaneous, as Swedenborgism became associated with the Romantic tradition.

But the first part of the symbolist story is primarily French, for it was Baudelaire who bridged the gap between the Romantic treatments of Swedenborgism and its eventual applications to the symbolist cult. Those who came to Paris with a common philosophical orientation were able by the end of the century to take symbolism out of the confines of French literature and bring it to its apotheosis as an international literary movement.

SWEDENBORGISM
AND THE
ROMANTICISTS

Swedenborg is the patron saint of too many ideologies, philosophies, and literary trends to qualify as the special property of symbolism. Any study of the literary backgrounds of nineteenth-century literature has specific allusions to the popularity of Swedenborgism as the basic mysticism of the time. When the Temple of Reason abolished official religion in France during the Revolution, the apocryphal doctrines of illuminism provided a convenient substitute for the unsuppressible metaphysical thirst. As Blake had explained in his *Marriage of Heaven and Hell,* it was not the originality of Swedenborg's theories that made it such an attractive cult, but rather Swedenborg's ability to sum up and popularize so many parallel mystical notions that were inherent in the cabbalistic and hermetic cults. According to Blake, not a single new truth was discovered by Swedenborg: his precepts had all been conceived earlier; his philosophy was a synthesis of all the occult philosophies of the past. In turn, the translations of Swedenborg into English, French, and German were so numerous that his ideas became common property and underwent the distortions that generally occur in the indiscriminate handling of abstractions by those who need the concrete example of the thought.

Proceeding from the biblical concept that man is made in the image of God, Swedenborg arrived at the conclusion that what is spirit in man already exists in its natural form, but needs redefinition in terms of existence after life. The proof of anterior and posterior existence was seen to lie in the inner consciousness of spiritual sensations as distinct from sensual perceptions: every natural, physical vision had its penumbra of spiritual recognition. This recognition had been, it was thought, more acute in primitive man; the spiritual signification of the physical had been spelled out through the Word—that is, by way of communication between the Divine being and man. But this intercourse was not *direct* communication; it occurred through symbols, i.e. phenomena in the physical world that had a dual meaning, one recognizable to the earthly perceptions of man, the other to his spiritual ones:

In a word, all things which exist in nature from the least to the greatest are correspondences. The reason they are correspondences is that the natural world with all that it contains exists and subsists from the spiritual world, and both worlds form the Divine being.[1]

Not only did God communicate with man in this fashion, but man communicated with heaven through these same correspondences:

The Word was written by pure correspondences as a means of union between heaven and man.[2]

And here is Swedenborg's definition of the Divine word as expressed in his *Heaven and Hell:*

If man has a knowledge of correspondences he would understand the Word in its spiritual sense and would obtain a knowledge of hidden truths of which he sees nothing in the

1 Emanuel Swedenborg, *Heaven and Hell* (New York: E. P. Dutton, 1911), p. 44.
2 *Ibid.,* p. 49.

sense of the letter. For in the Word there is a literal sense and there is a spiritual sense. The literal sense insists on such things as are in the world, but the spiritual sense of such things as are in heaven; and since the union of heaven with the world is effected by correspondences, therefore a Word was provided in which everything down to the minutest detail has its correspondence.[3]

It is strange that, in the midst of the Age of Enlightenment, such literal enunciation of immortality should have become a popular philosophy. It is highly obvious that from the beginning the influence of Swedenborg on aesthetics was primarily verbal rather than conceptual. Even as the terminology was being adopted by literary men, the meanings given to it were varied and contradictory—and thus symptomatic of an inherent criticism of the philosophy.

The one meaning in Swedenborgism that no one accepted was the definition of symbol. When Swedenborg says that "garden" means wisdom, "trees" are the knowledge of good, "bread" is affection, this is old-fashioned allegory and not *symbol,* as the word evolved in the century following Swedenborg. A direct application of Swedenborgism would strive toward order and clarification in a world of confusion and mystery. The entire history of literature from Romanticism to symbolism and on to surrealism is, on the contrary, indicative of man's shunning of order and his cult of the mystery of things unknown rather than of a desire to associate illumination with order or rationality.

Emerson read Swedenborg as early as the 1830's. His essay on *Nature* (1836) bears the imprint of the philosophy of correspondences. He views language as a body of signs mediating between concrete realities on earth and their spiritual counterparts in heaven. It is true that after his visit to Manchester in 1847 he chastised the philosopher for his lack of a sense of beauty and poetry: "it is remarkable that this man who, by his perception of symbols saw the poetic con-

3 *Ibid.,* pp. 49–50.

struction of things, and the primary relation of mind and matter, remained entirely devoid of the whole apparatus of poetic expression, which that perception creates." However, his Transcendentalism leaned heavily on Swedenborgian philosophy and was to create a whole lineage in American literature concurrently with Symbolism abroad. The mystique of Swedenborg, subjected to poetic mutations, was then to make a full circle and return to Europe via the Poe-Baudelaire relationship.

A more substantial criticism of Swedenborgism appears in William Blake's *Marriage of Heaven and Hell*. The important word there is "marriage," which speaks in favor of the spirit of conciliation Blake found inherent in the concept that Swedenborg had represented as an antithesis. Early in the book Blake calls on the resources of "hell," which he defines as energy, as well as on those of "heaven," which is reason, to achieve a sense of the infinite. He aspires to the knowledge of the absolute through a deeper enjoyment of the senses, rather than through their purification, and through the abolition of the duality of soul and body. *The Marriage of Heaven and Hell* is not a product of influence so much as it is a criticism of Swedenborg's *Heaven and Hell*. Blake was far out in his notion of poetry, if not in his poetic expression. Whereas the Romanticists accepted the famous concept of duality and wove their imagery around that vision of existence, it is clear from Blake's attitude toward Swedenborg that Blake's sphere of influence was to be among the modernists rather than among the Romanticists or the Symbolists, although his name often appears in reference to both those literary schools.

The important fact that emerges out of these ambiguities of influence is that, in the history of aesthetics during the past two hundred years, we find the same words—"analogy," "correspondence," "infinite," "absolute," "dream," and a number of others—used in at least three different senses. A comprehension of these differences of meaning of the rather limited vocabulary that we use to describe the "poetic" is essential to an understanding of the frontiers of symbolism. Otherwise, we reduce three different poetic concepts to a single form, and all literary criticism that attempts to discriminate among styles becomes mere redundance.

True, all poetry since the beginning of the Romantic movement has appropriated the domain of the mystical as a kind of substitute for religion: the Romanticists sought analogies or intimations of the infinite; so did the symbolists; and so did the surrealists. A book on Romanticism will tell us that the true Romanticist found his vista in the dream, as the intermediary stage between this world and the next; but so did the symbolist cultivate dreams as the only vital level of existence of the poet, and the surrealist probed the dream world not merely to enjoy the state but thereby to cultivate the possibilities of his mind. The same cult— but for different reasons! The Romanticist aspired to the infinite, the symbolist thought he could discover it, the surrealist believed he could create it; thus the word "infinite" meant something different to each. If we dwell on this aspiration to the absolute to sum up the aims of these three literary schools, we seem to be reducing them to a single pattern—but this is true only until we examine the works themselves and realize that we cannot juxtapose a poem by Shelley, one by Verlaine, and one by Breton, even if we use a single terminology to verbally express their poetic purpose. In effect, symbolism would have to be considered just a continuation of Romanticism unless it could be established that its comprehension of the expression "correspondence" was quite different from that of the Romanticists. For that reason, the study of symbolism will not be conducted in these pages on a plane of literary isolation, but in relation to the other two basic poetic movements—Romanticism and surrealism—with an awareness of their common share in the heritage of the illuminists and hermetics, and the different literary fortunes they each made out of it.

⊙

In France one of the most vivid applications of Swedenborgism by the Romantic writers was that of Balzac's *Livre mystique,*[4] a volume in a trilogy of novels in which characters who have become fascinated by the teachings of Swedenborg search for communication with the Master here on earth and are eventually transcended into that state which Swedenborg had said was lost to man when he became spiritually maimed in evolved society. These books have often been taken to indicate a passing stage in the formation of the "realist" that Balzac is considered to have become with the writing of the *Comedie humaine.* Today there is much doubt as to whether the label "realist" really did Balzac justice—unless it was used in the particular sense attributed to it by the head of the Realist school, Champfleury: "Family of restless dreamers, seekers of the unexpected."

If Balzac's trilogy, entitled *Recherche de l'Absolu,* is taken as a phase in the continuity of his vision and orientation, rather than as a curious, exceptional moment, the whole work can be viewed quite differently, as one of the most illuminating examples of Romanticism in France, more Romantic than most of the poetry of Balzac's contemporaries in France, and constructed along the lines of the pattern with which Swedenborg contemplated the gamut of existence: Heaven and earth, the Divine and the human. The *Recherche de l'Absolu* is Balzac's version of the Divine comedy,

[4] It is obvious that the Symbolists considered Balzac one of theirs when one sees that Arthur Symons includes him in his book *The Symbolist Movement in Literature,* Yeats writes of him in symbolist context, and Ernest Dowson writes a poem called "Seraphita Seraphitus." This is not to mention all the allusions to Balzac among the French symbolists.

whereas the rest of the work is the human, graceless
comedy of those who have become circumscribed
within the confines of earthly desires and have lost the
connections with the divine that were manifest in
Seraphita and Louis Lambert, the mystical characters
of the *Recherche de l'Absolu.*

Balzac had read Swedenborg in abridged form in
his mother's library, where there were many books on
mysticism, and he had stated in no uncertain terms
that "Swedenborgism is my religion." To crystallize the
notion of an intermediary who may be in touch with
both heaven and earthly existence, he invented that
most Romantic of all fictional characters: Seraphitus
or Seraphita, the uncertainty of the name-ending in-
dicating the uncertainty of sex, or the unisex of heavenly existence, where the processes of reproduction
are no longer necessary. He or she is a seventeen-year-
old "monster," a monster in the Romantic sense of the
word, i.e. not natural. He is a cousin of Swedenborg,
subject to hallucinatory states in which he can communicate both with the living and the spirits, thereby
living on the frontiers of both the visible and the invisible. He will, of course, not be able to maintain the
delicate balance between the rational and irrational,
and he will eventually enter into a state of complete
insanity. But before doing this, he will communicate
with the couple Mina and Wilfred, who represent
ideal, earthly love; the overtones of their love is identified with the spiritual world to which they aspire.
When Seraphita explains to Mina and Wilfred the
eventual unity of things in the hereafter, Balzac acts
as a spectator, or descriptive agent, just as he will
later in the *Comédie humaine,* when he is commenting
on the earthly mores of humans. When Seraphita indicates that part of this unity consists of the intermingling of the sense perceptions that here on earth are
divided and separated, Balzac's comment is: "Many
good minds do not admit these worlds where

colors make delightful concerts heard, where words
kindle. . . ." If this is a suggestion of synesthesia, it is
not at all what the symbolists later meant by it. The possibility of this intermingling of sense perceptions is
clearly relegated by Balzac to the hereafter. It is Seraphita's promise to the young couple, rather than something that can be achieved here and now. Moreover,
Seraphita's promise of unity is a divine rather than a
human promise. The duality accepted during human
existence will revert to a unity in God in the eventual
unity of all sensations: "They understood the invisible
bonds by which material worlds were attached to
spiritual worlds." This is the comprehension of duality
by humans before they have reached the next step
Continuing, we find:

In remembering the sublime efforts of the most beautiful
human geniuses, they found the principle of melody upon
hearing the choirs of heaven which gave sensations of color,
perfume, thought and which recalled the innumerable details of all creation, as an earthly song revives infinite
memories of love.

When Seraphita says: "Believe me, miracles are in
us and not outside of us," it is again in reference to the
knowledge that the human mind may strive to attain
of the relationship between the outside world and the
divine. It is in this sense that numbers are said to have
meanings, and the smallest flower represents a thought.
Again, let us note that the *thought* is more important
than the *flower,* and the appreciation of the earthly
sensation is significant only in so far as it throws light
on the understanding of the divine. This is the meaning of "correspondences" in terms of the Romantic
vision, and, as will be seen, it is a far cry from the
symbolists' comprehension of the same word and its
illustrations.

What must be the attitude of the man who envisages
creation in this light? One of retreat from the world,

an attitude of exile. And if the poet is, of all men, best able to foresee the correspondences, he is to be by the same token the most withdrawn from the world, the most awkward in the performance of purely human activities. The very pertinent image by which this status is expressed is in that very Romantic poem of Baudelaire called "L'Albatros," in which the bird is seen to fly in exquisite grace and sense of compatibility in the skies, but loses its ease and affinity with the environment when it is brought down to earth by the hunter's arrow. He is awkward on land, i.e. on earth, he who was so free and happy in the skies, i.e. in heaven.

The Romantic poet's movement is one of constant ascent through what Wordsworth called "the earth apparelled in celestial light." The means for this ascent is a recurrent effort to achieve moral purification and the appreciation of the beauties of earth, which provides a constant reminder that they are but the symbols of what is in store. In "Dieu," the philosophical poem that Victor Hugo wrote late in his career, but still under the aegis of Romanticism, we find in the poet's dialogue with God that the consent to know the infinite becomes a consent to die; the last words of the poem are "Et je mourus," as he comes full face with the vision. In the case of Balzac's Seraphita, the consequence of the celestial vision is insanity. In other Romantic works, the vision of the supernatural is attained through the effects of intoxicants, and, best of all, through the dream state. We can say that if the Romantic seeks the dream state, it is as a makeshift for the celestial vision while he is detained here on earth.

Again, in Balzac we find a close implementation of Swedenborg's philosophy when he defines for us the prototype of this sort of dreamer in the characterization of Louis Lambert. A young man of twenty-eight, he too will end in insanity. But before he loses complete contact with reality—as we generally define reality—we follow him into that intermediary stage in which the gradual loss of the real and involvement in the dream are like the changing proportions in an hourglass, hardly perceptible as they occur. In the double life he leads, there is at first a fifty-fifty proportion between interior and exterior actions, but little by little the interior overpowers the exterior life. The dream becomes such a powerful dose of opium that Lambert is overwhelmed by the conviction that the inner faculties are not dependent on outside stimuli. Balzac defines a new faculty of the thinking process that makes him designate Louis Lambert as a "voyant."

Here we have another of those ambiguous terms that are going to mean different things to different people. Translated simply as "seer" or "visionary," it came to refer to visionaries as diverse as Fourier and Rimbaud, Hindu philosophers, and opium eaters. For Balzac, the visionary is pretty much what he was for Swedenborg: the human being who is equipped with vision more rapid than sequential thought and who can therefore grasp the totality of the object or phenomenon before the sequence and relationship of the parts are consciously understood. This is the sense of what other Romanticists have called "ecstasy," but it is not what Baudelaire will mean by the same word, nor what Rimbaud will popularize as the *clef de touche* of surrealism. We shall reexamine the word as we come to it in other contexts. In Balzac the "voyant" is definitely a master of the abstract, since all vision of the celestial is conceived in terms of abstractions. The cult of the marvelous can be achieved only through this power of superconcept, according to the story of Louis Lambert; of course, whoever has this faculty will be ostrasized in this world, misunderstood and unloved:

Flower born on the edge of an abyss, it had to fall unknown even as its colors and its perfumes were unknown. Like many misunderstood people, had he not often wished to plunge without conceit into nothingness, to lose in the mael-strom the secret of his life?

⊙

The German poets who were the predecessors of the French Romanticists were much more susceptible to the cult of the dream, the magic of imagination, religious sincerity, and escape into the world of the spirit than were the French poets.[5] At first mentioned, but little read, in France, the German Romanticists became more available in translation by the middle of the nineteenth century. The vocabulary which was to become the common pool of all aesthetic mysticism was first used by the Germans and then in reference to them by their admirers outside of Germany.[6] Was it used, however, in the Romantic sense or the Symbolist sense?

Jean-Paul was a "visionary" according to Mme. de Stael, who was the first to alert the French to the wonders of the Nordic imagination. Jean-Paul wrote three works dealing with the world of the imaginary—*Über die natürliche Magie der Einbildskraft* (1796), *Über das Träumen* (1799), *Blicke in die Traumwelt* (1814)—in which the concept of "Je est un autre" (I is another), which will later become Rimbaud's "orig-inal" wording of the relationship between the author and his work, is already manifest. The poet is the ob-jective spectator of his working self. This is likened to the state of man during a dream, and therefore the

5 For a detailed and perceptive discussion of the cult of the dream in German Romantic poetry see Albert Béguin, *L'Ame romantique et le rêve* (third ed.; Paris: Corti, 1963).

6 The philosophical rather than the literary approach to the notion of the symbol, which is revealed in the prose writings of Schlegel and Schilling and has its foundation in German philos-ophy, is admirably discussed in René Wellek's *A History of Modern Criticism,* Vol. II (New Haven: Yale University Press, 1955). This book sheds light on the mystical reorientation that had to take place in the nineteenth-century mind before its literary reflections could be discerned.

poetic act is compared to the act of dreaming. Jean-Paul wrote:

> The real poet in writing is only an auditor, not the master of his characters; that is to say that he does not compose the dialogue by piecing together the answers, according to a spiritual stylistics which he has learned painfully. But as in the dream, he watches his characters come to life, *he listens.*[7]

Jean-Paul supposed the dream to contain both Heaven and earth and saw it as characteristic of the full comprehension of the duality of existence. His nostalgia for the "Golden Age" is akin to the Swedenborgian sense of the loss of a world in which the correspondences were understood and communicated. There is a definite barrier between the self that dreams and the self that lives, and no consistent techniques are developed in his poetry to bridge the gap or to show the flow from the one to the other.

When Franz von Baader speaks of the "internal sense," we have a rewording of Swedenborg's notion of the independence of spiritual sensations from outside stimulation. The objective "obscurity" of such imagery is produced, according to Baader, through omission of the link between the inner image and the outer world. The artist, according to him, is the man who is illuminated by these inner perceptions and is therefore withdrawn from outside impressions: "It is the inner sense, and not the one that copies the exterior which illuminates the progress of genius." He concludes from this that the artist is "a seer or a visionary." [8] This definition of the visionary is very similar to Balzac's, as it encompasses strictly inner visions produced through mental abstractions. On the same notion, so persistent in German poetry at the time, J. W. Ritter writes to Franz von Baader: "everything we imagine

[7] Jean-Paul as quoted in Béguin, *op. cit.*, p. 189.
[8] Franz von Baader as quoted in Béguin, *op. cit.*, p. 75.

is real" [9]—real in terms of the correspondence with the world beyond, the "half-reality of which the other half is the sacred." And since the dream is closer to the spiritual world, because of its lesser dependence on outside stimulus, then, according to this reasoning, in sleep man is closer to the universal reality. The dream is thus, in effect, involuntary poetry. But let us not forget that all this antedates Freud, and that the word "reality" is being used in the sense of the divine, unattainable here and now, in concordance with the definition of Champfleury, who identified the realist with the dreamer. With the rejection of the outside world, the duality remains quite distinct between the natural and the supernatural; the problem of the relationship possible to establish between the inner man and the outer world is in no way so significant as the relationship between the inner world of man and the world of the hereafter. This perspective links Jean-Paul, Franz von Baader, and other Germans of the period much more closely with the spirit of the Romantics than with that of the Symbolists who follow, even though their writings—and particularly their reputation as mystics—were to be significant in Symbolist circles.

In the case of Gotthilf Heinrich von Schubert, Brentano, Novalis, Tieck, and Hoffmann, there was a clearer orientation toward what was to become the Symbolist aesthetics, as the barriers between the inner and outer vision became more pliable. Schubert's first attempt at a definition of symbolism was "concentrated verbalization." In *Symbolik des Traumes* (1814), he saw the need for a new use of language to express succinctly the relationships between the abstract and the concrete. He realized what some of his German contemporaries could not see, and what his French readers of a generation later were to grasp—that the symbol

---

[9] J. W. Ritter as quoted in Béguin, *op. cit.*, p. 76.

must not be an abstraction, but must be conceived in terms of physical imagery. Yet, Schubert's premonition did not survive in effective illustrations, for he, like his colleagues, was too deeply impressed by Swedenborg's allegories. Although he expressed a nostalgia for a lost harmony, when he tried to decipher the keys of the universe in terms of images, he fell into pat correspondences between colors and qualities—yellow for mourning, red for joy, etc. There was to be, in fact, a whole series of "yellow" imagery in the Swedenborgian manner among the late Romanticists, such as Sainte-Beuve's *Les Rayons jaunes* and Tristan Corbière's *Les Amours jaunes*.

Ludwig Tieck's awareness of the relationships between things that seem so far apart brings us closer to that interplay between the inner and the outer image which was to be at the heart of the Symbolist aesthetics. His was a major step toward a poetic relationship other than the one between Heaven and earth, and created by a sense of fantasy rather than by the rational explanation of the spiritual bonds with Heaven. Although considered the head of the Romantic School, Tieck seems to deviate markedly from the *Sturm und Drang* tradition when he warns that emotions must never be too violent in the dream, lest they mar the illusion created by the images. It is also true that, in their concern for the dream, both Schubert and Tieck mentioned the prophetic dream—which is closer to Rimbaud's notion of the visionary than to Swedenborg's. This does not by the same token bring their concept closer to the Symbolists' handling of the dream, but it does mark a deviation from the Romantic pattern.

Novalis also foresees the symbolist movement when he suggests that poetry in its broad allegorical meaning can have indirect effects even as music ("indirekte Wirkung wie Musik,") and poetry as incantation provides comprehension on the "illuminated" level

("Durch Poesie entsteht die höchste Sympathie und Koaktivität,[10] die innigste Gemeinschaft des Endlichen und unendlichen") [11] However, in *Die Lehrlinge zu Sais* (1798), when Hyacinth arrives at the temple of Sais, he is confronted with a *veiled* statue of Isis and hears admonitions that no mortal can lift the veil—a notion that approximates Victor Hugo's "Et je mourus." It is interesting to note that Yeats' title for the part of his autobiography which encompasses the symbolist years is *The Trembling of the Veil*, suggested to him by Mallarmé; [12] here is an appropriate modification of the image, for if the "veil" represented a barrier to the Romanticists, the "trembling of the veil" suggests to the symbolist a movement, if not outright withdrawal of the obstacle.

The relationship between inner and outer perception is even more marked in the writing of Achim von Arnim and E. T. A. Hoffmann. The frontiers between the dream and reality become more blurred, so that what we have here is in truth a projection of the inner state onto the objective reality. But if this is true ipso facto, and the examples could be multiplied in Arnim's tales and in Hoffmann's *Kreisleriana* and *The Golden Vase,* there is yet no awareness of the possibility of creating a technique to verbalize this interplay. There is explanation of the state, in *direct discourse,* rather than a self-contained representation of it. When Hoffmann says that hearing is a more perfect form of seeing, the writer is making a communication about his experience, but the reader is not discovering the phe-

10 The double meaning of the word suggests the use of the word "Co-Naissance" by Claudel in similar perspective.

11 Cf. Frederick Hiebel, *Novalis* (Chapel Hill: University of North Carolina Press, 1954).

12 In his preface Yeats explains the origin of his title: "I have found in an old diary a saying from Stephane Mallarmé that his epoch was troubled by the trembling of the veil of the Temple. As those words were still true, during the years of my life described in this book, I have chosen *The Trembling of the Veil* for its title."

nomenon through the poetic communication itself. The same comment can be made about the explanation of synesthesia by Hoffmann, who tells us that when he heard a great deal of music the relationships between colors, sounds, and perfumes became evident and mingled in a màrvelous concert. This is not a communicated or shared experience, but the recording of an experience, which the reader is expected to accept on the word of the author. There is no new *symbolistic* technique here but an explanation of what symbolist writing might explore. In the German Romanticists we have not yet reached symbolist writing, but we have located the terrain that is to be cultivated by it.

⊙

Swedenborgism was to become a fad before it became an influence, if by "influence" we mean not imitation, but *mutation*, application, transformation, springboard to new creation. As Enid Starkie describes in her book on Baudelaire, the Swedenborg fad or convention resulted in perfume concerts, such as Thore's in France in 1852, and books on the art of perfume, including one by Etienne Souriau and M. Frankel entitled *Gammes des parfums,* in which it was suggested that "there is no reason why smell art lovers should not meet like music lovers at a concert." Alphonse Karr expounded the correspondences between colors and abstract qualities. And finally, at the Exposition of 1855, there was an immense keyboard of correspondences.[13]

In fine, the influence of Swedenborg on Romanticism, over and above fads and popularizations, made a deep impression on the Romanticists' commitment to divine existence. The natural world is at the same time a barrier and a scale of symbols of the divine.

[13] Cf. Enid Starkie, *Baudelaire* (New York: New Directions, 1958), p. 235.

Only through recognition of the duality between our spirit and our senses could the poet approach the eventual unity in the hereafter. The multiplicity of our senses was to be seen only as an indication of the synesthesia that would occur in the unifying process of celestial life: The dream as well as all other irrational states were interventions of the divine and previews of the infinite. The Romanticists espoused Swedenborg's notion that the visionary quality in man was a superrefinement of his thought process, rather than Blake's avant-garde position that it rose out of an intensification of sensory acuteness. The elimination of the distinction between body and soul was not attainable here and now, as Blake had supposed in his criticism of Swedenborg. Nor was the higher enjoyment of the sensual the desired end; rather, it was the withdrawal as much as possible from outside stimuli that brought the visionary into the purest forms of the poetic state.

In the following chapters it will be seen how the same basic philosophy and the same mystical words came to mean different things as they became part of the ideals and the terminology of symbolism.

III

BAUDELAIRE

In view of the cult of the notion of correspondences in the Romantic era, it becomes all the more strange and astonishing that Baudelaire's little sonnet on the "Correspondances" should have been hailed by later poets as a milestone, and a fountainhead for symbolism. Every book on Baudelaire brings out the *fact* of the influence of Swedenborg on this sonnet. It has also been pointed out that "nature is a temple" was a verity perceived by such sundry and varied persons as Plutarch, Montaigne, Gassendi, Diderot, Robespierre, Edgar Allan Poe, Chateaubriand, and Ruskin.

Baudelaire's one abortive attempt at writing a novel produced *La Fanfarlo,* in which he fashioned a hero, Samuel, who much resembles Balzac's Louis Lambert. Baudelaire places a volume of Swedenborg at the hero's bedside. Thereafter, whenever Baudelaire is mentioning correspondences—and there is much mention of this subject in his critical writings—it is in connection with his concept of Romanticism that he makes the reference. It is never suggested by Baudelaire that he is inventing something that is different from the concept of the Romanticists, or that he is proposing to fashion a new way of writing based on the notion. In truth, it is the most exciting aspect of the birth of literary movements that their real originators are rarely aware of having accomplished anything extraordinary. Baudelaire was not conscious of having done anything but verbalize upon a philosophic precept. Nowhere in his many autobiographical comments is

there the slightest indication that he thought "Correspondances" a great, or even a significant poem. Certainly, in his own time, "La Charogne" was much more
famous. And Victor Hugo never specified exactly what
was the "frisson nouveau" that he detected in Baudelaire's poetry.

The best indication we have that Baudelaire did not
consider himself to be the creator of a new form of
aesthetics is the obvious fact that his allusions to "symbolism" were made in reference to authors whom we
consider today to be quite remote from the symbolist
way of writing and the *symbolist* *mystique*. He says
the same thing about Hugo and Gautier—that they
deciphered the universal analogy. In his article on
"Theophile Gautier" in *L'Art romantique* he observes:

If one reflects that to this marvelous faculty Gautier adds
an immense inner intelligence of the universal correspondence and symbolism, that repertory of all metaphors, one
can understand that he can increasingly, indefatigably and
unerringly define the mysterious attitude that the objects of
creation hold before man's eyes. There is in the word, in
the *Verb,* something *sacred* which forbids us to make of it a
game of chance. To handle a language wisely means to
practice a kind of evocative witchcraft.[1]

In his description of the genius of Hugo, he makes of
him a disciple of Swedenborg, giving as evidence the
magnificent repertory of analogies and metaphors that
link the human with the divine—unequalled, as he
says, except in the Bible. He goes on to generalize that
the poet, in the broad definition of the word, is a trans-
lator, a decipherer of the divine hieroglyphics. He
also accepts the literal correspondence between the
divine and natural worlds. This brings his notion of
the symbol very close to the concept of allegory and

1 The quotations from the works of Baudelaire used in this
chapter are from Baudelaire, *Oeuvres complètes* (Paris: Bibliothèque de la Pléiade, 1954).

to the traditional parallelism between the abstract and the concrete. In fact, Baudelaire defines Romantic art in terms of the famous duality and its representation in poetic imagery. When in "Le Poème du haschisch" he talks of "l'intelligence de l'allégorie," he means the understanding of what, in the article on Hugo, he spoke of as the practically mathematical exactitude of the correspondence. It is quite clear that in Baudelaire's mind there is no real distinction between allegory and symbol. The same Swedenborgian yardstick is applied to Poe in Baudelaire's preface to *Nouvelles Histoires extraordinaires* when he says: "It is this admirable, this immortal instinct of the Beautiful which makes us consider the earth and its spectacles as a vision, a correspondence of Heaven."

It is true that Baudelaire is a fountainhead for the symbolist movement, but his influence is based on much more than his use of the terminology of Swedenborg in an isolated sonnet and its reiteration in his description of the Romantic poets of France.

Before pinning down "influences," one must recognize that Baudelaire's most salient characteristic is his diversity, his very lack of a salient trait, his virtual reversibility and multiplicity of character. The student of literary criticism could go through his verse and prose writings and find enough substantiation, compile enough quotes, to make him a Swedenborgian poet; after which, he could go back and find enough proof to arrive at a diametrically opposite conclusion. This complexity is, of course, precisely what makes Baudelaire an interesting personality, one about whom the critic can write endlessly; the facets are so many and so paradoxical. Historically, he is maladjusted; he comes too late and too early. What is accepted has been chewed over too much; yet, psychologically, the accepted is yet too popular to make a call to reaction against it effective.

Baudelaire, who is not a disinterested writer, who

is on the contrary passionately interested in being
accepted as a poet, in becoming recognized and famous,
pays court to the Hugos and the Gautiers and the
Sainte-Beuves who could so easily launch his career.
All the writing about Swedenborgism and its application to the stellar writers of his time represents the
official facet of Baudelaire. It is certainly not in that
aspect of his writings that we will find indications of
his break with tradition. He can add nothing but his
consent and his conformity to the inroads that Swedenborg made on the poetic vision; and Baudelaire's notion of correspondences is definitely in the Romantic
tradition and had already been beautifully paraphrased for the French from the writings of the master
himself by Mme. de Staël. If we are to judge the symbolist style and the symbolist movement as something
other than the continuation and redundance of Romanticism, it is certainly not in the Swedenborgian
influence that we are going to locate its originality.

As a matter of fact, Baudelaire, almost in spite of
himself, deviates from his adherence to Swedenborgian
mysticism. In two important instances he contradicts
Swedenborg while using the philosopher's own terminology. In his dedicatory poem of *Les Fleurs du
Mal* he addresses the reader as "hypocrite lecteur" in
the sense in which Swedenborg used the term, i.e. of
men who have spoken like angels but who have in-
wardly acknowledged nature alone. Baudelaire, however, also calls the reader "mon semblable, mon frère,"
thereby implying that perhaps the transcendence of
which he will give some indications in some of his
poems may be a pretense; and in betrayal of the patron
saint of the literary men of his time, the spiritual experience which he will communicate in his neatly contrived anthology is really circumscribed within nature's
earthly limitations. It is interesting to note that many
years later T. S. Eliot borrowed the entire expression

from Baudelaire in *The Waste Land* and used it right after casting doubt on the notion of resurrection: a tacit nod of confirmation from Eliot to Baudelaire!

Succinctly, Baudelaire tantalizes the reader from the very start of *Les Fleurs du Mal;* for every poem of transcendental inspiration, there is one that contents itself with "l'expansion des choses infinies," i.e. the infinite in terms of material things, or the inner abyss rather than the supraterrestrial elevation. Again, at the very end of *Les Fleurs du Mal,* at the close of "Le Voyage" (the last of the six poems grouped under the heading of "La Mort"), Baudelaire seems to be giving an answer to Swedenborg when he protests against the duality of the infinite by suggesting: "Enfer ou ciel, qu'importe!" And in the last lines:

Plonger au fond du gouffre, Enfer ou Ciel, qu'importe?
Au fond de l'Inconnu pour trouver du *nouveau!*

does not imply the idealization of the "vivants piliers" but rather the risk of perdition.

Now he believes, now he does not; now he soars with the ideal, now he plunges with the spleen; and if the sense of the transcendental makes him raise earthly images to the heights of immaterial spirituality, when he descends once again into his inner vision, he produces very material landscapes with his internal eye. Thus he is constantly tantalizing his reader, even as he is tormenting himself.

You can easily note the poems that emanate from these two contrary perspectives. When he is spiritualizing the material world, he gives us poems such as "Elévation," in which, referring to his mind, he says:

Envole-toi bien loin de ces miasmes morbides;
Va te purifier dans l'air supérieur,
Et bois, comme une pure et divine liqueur,
Le feu clair qui remplit les espaces limpides.

and later:

Heureux celui qui peut d'une aile vigoureuse
S'élancer vers les champs lumineux et sereins!

Celui dont les pensers, comme des alouettes,
Vers les cieux le matin prennent un libre essor,
—Qui plane sur la vie et comprend sans effort
Le langage des fleurs et des choses muettes!

In "Bénédiction" he describes the disorientation of
the poet on earth. He finds the taste of ambrosia and
nectar in all that he hears and drinks; he converses
with the wind and the sky; and he tolerates the jeers
of the public, for he knows that the purposes of his
being will transcend the disdain of his fellowmen:

Vers le ciel, où son oeil voit un trône splendide,
Le Poète serein lève ses bras pieux,
Et les vastes éclairs de son esprit lucide
Lui dérobent l'aspect des peuples furieux:

He says to God:

‹Je sais que vous gardez une place au Poète
Dans les rangs bienheureux des saintes Légions,
Et que vous l'invitez à l'éternelle fête.
Des Trônes, des Vertus, des Dominations.›

This is typical Romantic poetry; it represents the
official line, the ramifications of pure Swedenborgian
philosophy. The duality is expressed by the linking of
abstract qualities with concrete objects around the
poet; it is not the sort of duality that will lead to Symbolism, however.

But there is another duality in Baudelaire which
consists of the projection of the inner vision upon the
world without, situating the correspondence between
the inner vision and the outer reality, or in the interplay between the subjective and the objective. If we

examine "Correspondances" closely, we find that it is a contradiction in terms, containing an instance of disagreement with Swedenborg, even while Baudelaire is using the philosopher's own words. The sonnet actually contains two poems: the first part of it is the verbalization through direct statement of the Swedenborgian duality between the natural and the divine; but when we reach the last six lines, in which we would expect to find the implementation of that statement, Baudelaire sets out to disprove Swedenborg by means of a series of images—i.e. indirect discourse—cast on a plane of reality quite different from the vision of Swedenborg. The synesthesia that occurs in the mingling of sense perceptions does not produce a link between heaven and earth, nor does it transport us to a divine state; instead, it finds its connections between sense experiences here on earth: between perfumes and the flesh of children, linked by an adjective which has an olfactory as well as a tactical connotation, between sounds and colors (not in Heaven but here on earth) linking the oboe and the prairies, again through the clever use of an adjective that is applicable to more than one category of sensual imagery. In the last line, Baudelaire reveals that the secret of attaining synesthesia is not through the inner eye and its contact with the divine, but rather in the connection of the mind (*l'esprit*) with the senses (*les sens*) by means of a natural stimulus, such as incense or amber. The synesthesia is strictly earthly, descriptive of the kind of chain association that sensual stimuli can produce in the mind of man, and from which Proust was later to derive his notion of involuntary memory. Here the expansion of the sense stimulus does not go so far as to awaken a whole series of remembrances; what it does is to unleash metaphors on a double tract of sense perceptions. There is no spirituality here, even though most translators of Baudelaire's famous sonnet have used the English word "spirit" to transmit the concept of "esprit," thereby turning this rather sensual poem into a metaphysical one. It reached the Anglo-Saxon world in that guise, which helped to give "symbolist" poetry the metaphysical tinge that was later to be identified with those English poets who adopted the movement, and infused it with this somewhat erroneous interpretation of the Baudelairean interpretation of "correspondences."

Stefan George's German rendition suffered from the same incomplete translation of the notion of "expansion" and "esprit," which became "Hauch" (breath) and "Seelen" (soul), conveying neither the infinite meaning of things nor the mind's inherent powers to grasp them:

Mit einem hauch von unbegrenzten dingen
Wie ambra moschus und geweihter qualm
Die die verzückung unsrer seelen singen [2]

It is very rarely indeed that Baudelaire uses the expression "esprit" in its spiritual sense. He was an intellectual and sensual poet; this is in fact the basic distinction between him and his Romantic contemporaries. The mind sets the key to the poem, and the senses fill it with their harmonies. Affective vocabulary is at a minimum. In 1856, in a letter to Alphonse Toussenel, Baudelaire clearly defined the priority he gave to the type of imagination which is an intellectual rather than an emotional evidence of poetic creation:

I have been saying for a very long time that the poet is supremely intelligent, that he is intelligence itself—and that imagination is the most scientific of all faculties, because it alone understands universal analogy, or what mystic religion calls "correspondences."

But the type of intelligence he describes has to do with an entirely different set of analogies, and not the

[2] Stefan George, *Die Blumen des Bösen* (Berlin: G. Bondi, 1930).

correspondences of Swedenborg or the resulting transcendentalism of a poem such as "Elévation." When a unilateral externalization of the inner mood occurs, rather than an elevation, then we are indeed at the origins of Symbolism. For instance, in the poem "L'Ennemi" he likens his youth to a storm intermingled with brilliant sunshine, which leaves but a few ripe fruits behind it in his summer garden; having arrived at the "autumn of ideas," he wonders whether he can still till the inundated soil of his aging mind and dare to hope that it will provide the mystical nourishment for future flowers. This personification of the mind through the manifestations of nature is indeed the language of future symbolism. It is on a level that is somewhat obvious and still too close to allegory to be considered as actual Symbolism, but it sets the aesthetic direction which the Symbolist movement will take.

"Harmonie du soir," which comes in *Les Fleurs du Mal* right after one of the spiritualized Romantic poems, "L'Aube spirituelle," handles its symbolism with much more subtlety; in technique and perspective it proves to be, in fact, one of the genuine models of symbolist poetry, although chronologically it is avantgarde in terms of the Symbolist movement. Although this is a very well known poem, and much quoted in all kinds of context, it is fitting to quote it here in its entirety, in order that the discussion of its symbolist qualities may be more significant:

Voici venir les temps où vibrant sur sa tige
Chaque fleur s'évapore ainsi qu'un encensoir;
Les sons et les parfums tournent dans l'air du soir;
Valse mélancolique et langoureux vertige!

Chaque fleur s'évapore ainsi qu'un encensoir;
Le violon frémit comme un coeur qu'on afflige;
Valse mélancolique et langoureux vertige!
Le ciel est triste et beau comme un grand reposoir.

Le violon frémit comme un coeur qu'on afflige,
Un coeur tendre, qui hait le néant vaste et noir!
Le ciel est triste et beau comme un grand reposoir;
Le soleil s'est noyé dans son sang qui se fige.

Un coeur tendre, qui hait le néant vaste et noir,
Du passé lumineux recueille tout vestige!
Le soleil s'est noyé dans son sang qui se fige . . .
Ton souvenir en moi luit comme un ostensoir!

What are the symbolist elements in this poem? Before trying to answer that question, let us see of what Romantic ingredients it has divested itself. First, there is no direct statement of the poet's emotions: whatever we sense of the condition of his feelings comes to us through the indirect discourse of the imagery. Second, there is no transcendentalism: the memory which is evoked through the perfume is contained within the physical confines of the perfume itself; there is no parallelism between the physical state and an ideal or heavenly vision, only the sun drowning in its own blood as a projection of the sinking of the poet's heart into its own abyss.

This is the process of indirect discourse in full play: not the direct expression of emotion by means of qualifying, descriptive adjectives, not the representation of the emotion through specific allegorical personifications, but rather the intervention of communication between the poet and the reader through an image or a series of images that have subjective as well as objective value. While their objective existence is unilateral, their subjective meaning is multidimensional, and therefore suggestive rather than designated: the censer, the altar, the monstrance, the violin, the blood. Poetry communicates through the intermediary of the image: as a river purges itself of debris in a lake and comes out looking quite different, so the propelling concept passes through the pool of the metaphor and comes out transfigured. It has to be deciphered if for some reason there is need to reduce it to prosaic meaning. The duality expressed is thus between the memory rising in the poet and the odors and sounds of the universe rising as the scent of incense in a temple. The trembling violin serves as a hyphen between the performer (the poet) and the material character of the passive wood that has been sensitized by the human imprint. The violin becomes the outer manifestation of the heart, presaging the many violin images to be used by poets from Verlaine to those of the Symbolist school, as well as many other images of musical instruments used in the same symbolist manner. The inner state of man, his sadness, is molded with nature's qualities.

Not only does this duality occur between the mood of the poet and the appearances of nature, but even the physical ingredient, the blood of the poet, is projected upon the physical sun without. But this is not the pathetic fallacy of the Romanticists. Instead of their sentimentalizations of physical nature, we have here an early example of what T. S. Eliot was to call "the objective correlative." Nature does not embrace the poet; it serves as an instrument for poetic expression. And its range is as variable and versatile as a musical scale, which makes it possible for the poet to abandon the rational sequence of thought for a structure so much less rational—that of music: theme and variation, statement and development.

The process will not always be as obvious as it is in Baudelaire's "Harmonie du soir," but this poem's very clarity of structure demonstrates the process better than if one were to come directly upon a poem by Mallarmé. Along with the simulation of musical structure, there is also in this poem a play on musical sound. This is an aspect of symbolism that the French Symbolist school will carry to extremes as it loses sight of the aesthetic purpose of its associations with music and is carried away by its fascination with the manifestations of its infinite combinations. We shall see

later how this preoccupation with the *form* of music
rather than with the concept of musical communication will prove to be one of the pitfalls of symbolism.

In "Harmonie du soir" Baudelaire exemplifies the
Symbolist poem; in some of his prose writings he explains the process through which the poet may create
a symbolist image. In "Le Poème du haschisch" he describes that type of human being who with the aid of
stimulants can arrive at the heights of the poetic state.
It is clear that, when Baudelaire in a state of complete
lucidity describes the power of vision that man can
achieve under the effects of hashish, he is not speaking
of any or every man. On the contrary, he is very explicit in his description of the man-poet of the future:
half-nervous, half-bilious; possessing a cultivated mind
trained in the perception of form and color and a
tender heart wearied by unhappiness; having a taste
for metaphysics and philosophy; endowed with a moral
sense and, above all, with a keenness of the senses.
Such a person placed under the effect of hashish will
receive the final infusion of his imagination, one that
will make him believe in his own divinity.

If you are one of these souls, your innate love of form and
color will find first of all an immense pasture in the first
stages of your intoxication. Colors will assume an unac-
customed energy and will enter your brain in victorious
intensity. Delicate, mediocre, or even bad paintings on the
ceilings will turn frightfully alive; the crudest wallpaper
in taverns will deepen like splendid dioramas. Gorgeously
contoured nymphs stare at you with big eyes, deeper and
more limpid than sky or water; characters of antiquity,
rigged in sacerdotal or military costumes, by simplest nods
will exchange solemn secrets with you in a look. The sinu-
osity of lines is a very clear language in which you read the
agitation and desire of souls. Meanwhile, there develops in
you the mysterious and temporary state of mind in which
the depth of life, jostled by its multiple problems, is revealed in its totality in the spectacle, no matter how natural
or trivial it may be, that is taking place before your eyes—

where the first object that strikes your eye becomes a speaking symbol. Fourier and Swedenborg, the former with his analogies, the latter with his correspondences, have become embodied in the vegetable and animal life which strike your eye, and instead of teaching you by voice they indoctrinate you by means of form and color. The understanding of allegory takes on in you such proportions as you would never have suspected; let us observe incidentally that this *genre* which is so *spiritual*—which awkward artists have led us to scorn, but which is in truth one of the most primitive and natural forms of poetry—is restored to its original power when intelligence is illuminated through intoxication. Hashish then spreads over all of life like a magical varnish; it colors it solemnly and its light penetrates to the most imponderable depths. Laced landscapes, fleeting horizons, perspectives of cities paled by the cadaverous lividity of a storm, or illuminated by the ardent warmth of setting suns; depths of space, allegory of the depth of time—the dance, the gesture or declamation of the actors, if you happen to be in a theatre—the first sentence that strikes your eye, if you happen to be before an open book—everything and anything, the universality of beings ranges itself before you with a new and unsuspected glory. Even grammar, arid grammar, becomes a kind of evocative witchcraft; words are resurrected, covered with flesh and bone, the substantive in its solid majesty, the adjective, transparent garment which clothes it and colors it like a glazing, and the verb, angel of movement, which sets the sentence into motion. Music, that other language, cherished both by the lazy and by deep minds that find in it the relaxation that comes through diversification of work—this music speaks to you, tells you the poem of your life. It becomes part of you and you mingle with it. It speaks of your passion, not in vague and indefinite terms, as when you are enjoying a nonchalant evening at the opera, but in a particularized manner, each movement matching a beat of your soul, each note transformed into a word, and the total poem entering your mind like a dictionary endowed with life.

The theories of both symbolism and surrealism are contained intrinsically in this magnificent passage from "Le Poème du haschisch," which describes the quali-

fications of the man who wants to be a poet: the subjects that must be his concern, the uses to which he
must put language, the affiliations of the literary form
with the other arts, and—most important of all—the
relationship that must exist between his mental preoccupations and external reality. Baudelaire shows
how that outer reality effects the closest correspondence with the inner life of the poet when it is incar-
nated in the structural forms of musical sounds.

The fact that Baudelaire is describing the effects of
intoxication is of no significance in relation to the
larger description of poetic receptivity, without which
a hallucination would have no aesthetic meaning. The
most curious element of the description is that, whereas
he makes specific reference to both Swedenborg and
his French disciple, Fourier, and to their system of
allegory, the impact of the poetic mind on outer reality, as he sees it, and the transformations it can achieve
thereby, are quite unlike the Swedenborgian correspondences.

Both the imagery of symbolism and that of surrealism are fomented here, as Rimbaud and Mallarmé
read this luminous document. Rimbaud's *Les Illuminations* is there in nucleus, with all the potential of
phantasmagoria—stark, concrete, and rationally frag-
mental. But, more pertinent to the present study, we
have the nymphs, palaces, symbolistic choreography,
fragile inner landscapes, the rehabilitation of classical
myths, the shadowy horizons, the nostalgia over time
and space, that were to become the substance of symbolist poetry. Baudelaire foresees the sensual character
of the water imagery that was to be so important in
symbolist poetry; he enumerates the whole gamut of its
variations: fountains, cascades, still waters, stagnant
ponds; the blue immensities of the sea; enchanting
crystal matched solely by those mirrors whose importance is second only to that of the water.

Baudelaire sums up the poetic process as follows: the stimulus affects the senses, the senses affect the mind; the result is language, brought together by a superrational vigilance of the mind. The poem emerges as a whole, without the poet's having consciously put it together. In this, Baudelaire's aesthetics is doubly stacked: the description of the poetic act will make him a precursor of the surrealists, while the poetic visions, themselves resulting from the poet's organization and stylization of the chaos of reality, will act as a springboard for symbolist imagery. This process of the transformation of reality gives the poet a sense of his own divinity, rather than an aspiration *toward* divinity; the definition of "voyant" is then not that of Swedenborg or Balzac, but rather that of a director or transformer of dreams, "architecte de mes féeries" as Baudelaire calls himself in the poem "Rêve parisien." [3] On the one hand he expresses the notion of "voyant," which Rimbaud will grasp and convey in his famous letter; [4] on the other hand Baudelaire also influences the neurasthenic poets of the Symbolist school, to whom it will suggest how, through the cult of the ego, one may raise the condition of *poet* to that of sage and mystic, giving to the concept of *cénacle* something more than the figurative meaning.

We can also see in the above passage that Baudelaire foresees the two uses to which the notion of "music" will be applied in poetry: the massive, sensual use, to assuage the poetic anguish and provoke the dream release; and the intellectual uses of music, considered as a form of nonobjective thinking, activating the mind to suggest rather than to dictate concepts and visions. Baudelaire himself is more drawn toward the *sources* of intellectual stimulation that can be derived

[3] Mallarmé re-echoes that poetry must be "architectural et prémédité."
[4] Letter of May 15, 1871, to Paul Demeny.

from musical form. From this point of view Mallarmé
will be closer to him than will Verlaine and the instrumentalists of the Symbolist school.

This implication is reinforced in Baudelaire's essay
on Richard Wagner. He was one of the few persons in
the audience of the first performance of *Tannhäuser*
who did not boo and hiss it off the stage. Ecstatic over
his discovery of Wagner, Baudelaire spent days after-
wards wandering from café to café in an effort to find
an orchestra which might once more perform what persisted in his mind's ear. The power of Wagner's music
matched on the auditory level the intoxication of a
hashish orgy. It stimulated the imagination, throwing
the mind into a dream state such as leads to clair-
voyance. As with hashish, the intoxication produced a
state of synesthesia, as sound suggested color.

Baudelaire marveled at Wagner's use of legend. He
realized that, whereas the French Romanticists had
developed a sense of the historical under the guidance
of Chateaubriand and Mme. de Staël, the result had
been a rational, even prosaic use of local color and historical detail. But Wagner's use of the past through
the cult of the legend had achieved an illuminated vision of an epoch, not rationally exact but suggestive
of a sequence of events that was entirely different from
that of historical narration. Wagner mingled pagan-
ism, Gothic legend, and Christianity, creating a plane
of reality which was mystical without being religious,
in a sense parallel to the hypnotic atmosphere created
with words by Edgar Allan Poe.

If in Poe's mysterious and irrational world Baudelaire had glimpsed the cult of verbalism, in Wagner
he discovered the mystical uses of music: *symbolism
that is not allegory,* since it leaves a gap to be filled by
the imagination of him who hears it. If the melodies
are deemed to be the personification of ideas, they
nevertheless leave the ultimate interpretations to each
man who experiences the phenomenon. This is, of

course, parallel to the effects of intoxicants, which, depending on the sensory and neurological make-up of the intoxicated, are as variable and personalized as those of music. Wagner was for Baudelaire the true artist, the complete artist, who in his combination of drama, poetry, music, and décor exemplified that attainment of the perfect interplay of the sense perceptions that was to be the ideal of the poet. Shortly before his death, Baudelaire wrote to Wagner of his admiration; one of the saddest aspects of the final tragic months of this frustrated poet's life was the silence that he met, not knowing that the letter had taken a long time reaching its destination and was to be answered too late, alas, for Baudelaire to learn that his praises had been appreciated.

In determining Baudelaire's contribution to the Symbolist movement, we touch upon one of the most difficult problems of literary criticism: the distinction between an "originator" and a "precursor." Because both these words are used with multiple connotations, and without precision, there can be no significance to our use of them, unless we define the particular meaning that we attribute to the terms in a given work or under particular circumstances. An "originator" or *"chef d'école"* is a *conscious,* often *militant* reformer, in terms of pronouncements and performance. There is a tremendous awareness of the break with tradition, coupled inevitably with disdain for and downright rejection of the literary forms of the past. With this goes a sense of leadership, and the creation of an *entourage* of disciples.

None of these characteristics fit the image of Baudelaire that has come down to us. Victor Hugo was an originator of the Romantic theater of France: he declared it, fought for it, surrounded himself with champions of the cause, stood erect and high among his followers, was conscious of performing a literary mission. In contrast, a solitary and phlegmatic man like Baudelaire did not have the traits of leadership. The differences between himself and his contemporaries in literature were due, thought Baudelaire, to default on his part, not to creative, willful deviations. Hugo had encompassed with magnificent sweep the historical and emotional gamut of man, the open pastures and the lofty skies and seas. Leconte de Lisle had taken what remained of the globe and familiarized his readers with the exotic. To Baudelaire were left the penumbras of the mind, along with the ugly tunnels and narrow alleys of urbanism. "Mal" does not mean only "evil" in French; in its *double entendre* it also means "anguish." *Les Fleurs du Mal* were in a sense Baudelaire's apology for delivering what was left over after others had taken the lion's share.

Originality is rarely a self-evident characteristic; it can be defined only in retrospect. A summit cannot declare itself; it is a summit only in relation to what is around the bend, in terms of its horizon. The disgruntled and frustrated Baudelaire was constantly seeking associations; he wished to be linked with the Romantic tradition although he was aware of having to deal with left-over themes. He had high praise for his predecessors; there was no overt decision on his part to break with them. Originators are not always as original as they think they are; and the truly original mind does not necessarily have the ability to conceptualize its notions into a theory and to promote that theory. Baudelaire is not a Symbolist, but supplies fuel to Symbolism; his contributions can be spelled out concretely as they apply (1) to the notion of *poet*, (2) to the concept of poetic form, and (3) to the crystallization of the symbolist archetype.

In his own personal behavior, as well as in his conception of the poet's function, Baudelaire altered the Romantic notion of the poet. Since the time of Homer, the poet had been deemed a bard, who interprets and extols human emotion and who is particularly effective when he glorifies the national heritage or idealizes the historical event. Baudelaire makes poetry an intellectual rather than an emotional activity, and in this light the poet assumes the character of a sage or seer, rather than of a bard. With his superior network of senses and perceptions, he is bent on deciphering, rather than conveying or communicating, the enigma of life. If communication is the universalization of the particular, whether this be in the personal life of the poet or in the historical life of the nation, then deciphering is the power to give a personal reality to universal problems and their mysteries. The personalizing of a universal verity often results, to be sure, in the mystification of the reader rather than in his clarification. It also lifts poetry to a more cosmopolitan level, since the universal problems that the poet seeks to decipher are those that remain after the local colors have all been washed away.

In many of his critical writings, Baudelaire brings out the virtues of the cosmopolitanism of others; little does he seem to realize that he is the most cosmopolitan poet of them all—which is perhaps the greatest factor in the world-wide popularity he has achieved in the century that has passed since his death. Nothing is "exotic" for Baudelaire, because the word "exotic" stands in contradiction to cosmopolitanism. In terms of universal concerns nothing is "exotic": the human condition is the only poetic dimension for Baudelaire. This is the point of view he will convey to the Symbolists who will become in the years of "the end of the century" the most denationalized group of writers that ever worked together, not only because they convened in Paris, but because of their concern with universal moods and unlocalized landscapes.

In speaking of Wagner, Baudelaire had drawn a distinction between history and legend; his unconscious definition was a far cry from Hugo's notion of legend. For Hugo, legend is simply poeticized history; for

Baudelaire, legend as perceived in Wagner is the creation of a new sequence of events that belies historical fact or becomes a yardstick applicable to many differing histories. The poet is not simply a more vivid historian, but an anti-historian, dealing not with the temporal but with the eternal—which is the most cosmopolitan of all subjects. He will not reconstruct history, as Hugo did, but transform it. There will be as little or as much relationship between the poet and his compatriots as the latter are capable of becoming interested in nontemporal existence and preoccupations. It has been observed that today French poetry is, of all poetries, the one that bears the least connection with the ethnic tradition and character of the soil on which it has been nurtured. This deviation begins with Baudelaire; it later becomes a distinguishing mark of the Symbolist school.

Unwittingly, Baudelaire contributed to *the symbolist notions of form* as well. It is an obvious truth that revolutions, political as well as ideological, occur where conditions are most apt to provoke rebellion. English and German Romanticism were in themselves sufficiently radical deviations from classicism to forestall further drastic breaks in tradition in their wake. But in France, particularly in regard to poetic form, the break had not been as pronounced as had been expected. When the Parnassians finally rebelled against French prosody they somehow missed the basic issue. They protested against the personal effusions of the Romanticists; they attacked the subjects of poetry rather than the means of conveying them; they objected to the directness of communication between the poet's "I" and the reader, and they thought that they could avoid this simplicity of projection of the subjective by venturing into the impersonality of passive description and abstract verbalization. Their efforts did not eliminate the obviousness of direct discourse, but resulted simply in changing the subject matter of that discourse.

Baudelaire saw the problem more astutely, not in all of his poems, but, as we have seen, in certain ones that convey meaning through images which assume the role of indirect statement: this is a development which will be the sine qua non of symbolist writing. Another aspect of indirect discourse that Baudelaire discovered, but rather too generously attributed to the poetry of Hugo and Gautier, was the evocative power of words, the ability to confer to words themselves the power of imagery. This is a field that the surrealists were to utilize much more adeptly and extensively than the symbolists, yet there are instances in symbolist writing where words serve as veritable objects through the multiple sensations they evoke, just as objects imply varying images, according to the eye and the memory of the one who perceives them.

It is particularly in his prose criticism and descriptions of the effects of drugs on human sensitivity, that Baudelaire comes closest to the technique of indirect verbal communication in poetry. He leads us to a new definition of poetry: *the poem becomes an enigma.* The multiple meanings contained in words and objects are ingredients of the mystery and mood of the poem. There is never the sense of triumph of comprehension; the message remains as ambiguous as it is succinct, like the visions that come in the dream state or in the midst of a drug orgy of the kind described by Baudelaire. Although the difference between the poetic and the narcotic state of acute perception is not stated by Baudelaire, it can be deduced: in the narcotic condition the will of the person is nullified, whereas in the poetic state the ambiguity is intended as a part of the process of construction of the poem-riddle. We shall see in the writings of Mallarmé the broad dimensions and ramifications that poetic communication can assume through an even more sophisticated manner of indirect statement.

Finally, synesthesia itself is involved in Baudelaire's notion of indirect discourse. It comes to mean something larger than the mingling of sense perceptions. In his essay on Wagner, Baudelaire tackles the notion of the integration of the art forms and thereby the possibility of a broader synesthetic mingling of sense stimuli; he also meditates on the power of music to provoke, through the stimulation of a single sense, a multi-sensory plane of imagery. The implications for poetry are that, if music can suggest more than one level of imagery, then words may be able to assume the same function as structured musical notes, creating beyond the description of a sensation the sensation itself, and even that complexity of sensations which we call a "mood." Through this flexibility of communication, poetry would become an art form closer to music than it had been heretofore.

The third category of the influences which Baudelaire had on symbolism is in the shaping of the *archetype of the "decadent,"* which in terms of personality identification is the most closely associated with the Symbolist movement. As far as the word itself is concerned, Baudelaire did not have much use for it. In a letter to Jules Janin he says: "It is a word that has become very convenient for ignorant pedagogues; we make a very vague use of it, behind which we shelter our laziness and our lack of real curiosity." Baudelaire would have been the last one to launch the "decadent" type intentionally. In truth, he thought of himself more as a dandy than as a "decadent." The dandy, so well depicted by Flaubert in *L'Education sentimentale,* was the mid-century image of the lazy, egocentric man approaching middle age, yet with no real achievements to his record; opportunist in affairs of the heart; well dressed, although somewhat eccentrically; bored, so bored, having experimented with all ideas and experi-

ences and having reduced them all to the same mean-
ingless void.

On the surface Baudelaire qualified perfectly as a
dandy, but there was something more to Baudelaire—
the rough draft of what later generations were to call
the "decadent," giving it a definition in terms of
aesthetics and philosophy rather than of morality.

To Baudelaire, the term is vague and steeped in
moral prejudice; to those who come later, the identification of Baudelaire with the "decadent" image will
be in recognition of something in Baudelaire that is
closer to their own make-up. Although he had a narcissus complex, as did the dandies of his own generation, his preoccupation with the "gouffre" puts his
concern with his personal destiny on a metaphysical
level. After him, there will be a bifurcation of this notion of "gouffre." On the one hand, it will be cultivated
by the surrealists as the location of the extraordinary
and infinite here-and-now within the range of human
experience; on the other hand, it will be the symbolists'
basis for concern with the macabre, the target of their
images of mortality. The abyss of the unknown is taken
to be diabolical and divine at the same time; he who is
concerned with it is as metaphysical in character—if his
preoccupation is with evil or with the grotesque—as he
would be if he occupied himself with a Swedenborgian
"good and pure." This association of the angelic and
the diabolical was something that Baudelaire observed
in Edgar Allan Poe; it is what Harry Levin in his book
on the American contemporaries of the Symbolists has
so aptly called *The Power of Blackness* and "its con-
tinual interplay with a not less pervasive sense of white-
ness."

After Baudelaire this obsession with the abyss will
become one of the chief characteristics of the mental
attitude of what was called "decadent," in a rather
private and arbitrary use of the word that virtually
redetermined its meaning. In other words, *all* devia-

tion from the normal, whether physical or spiritual, was to be the domain *par excellence* of poetry, just as such deviations had been in the main the connecting trait of the subjects that Baudelaire had chosen for his writing. Furthermore, if personal immortality is rejected, death becomes instead the frontline target of metaphysical meditations. The "gouffre" is the frontier between the visible and the invisible, the conscious and the unconscious, nonlife and the living; how far one can push beyond the accepted frontier and still come back to write about it, became the foremost poetic question after Baudelaire. For the "decadent," who has grown tired of all other experiences, the "gouffre" is the only fountainhead of novelty, although the dangers of the journey are multiple and evident. This flirtation with death, suggested by Baudelaire, and its representation in literary imagery, will be exploited by the symbolists as they assume more and more the character of the "decadent" and explore the Plutonian fields of the morbid and the lethal. Swinburne, one of the first translators of Baudelaire, was also a sponsor of the "decadent" with his beautiful poem "Proserpine," a shining star of the darkness.

One of the most persistent emblems of mortality in the symbolist frame of reference will be the Hamlet-figure: Hamlet contemplating the skull in the grave-diggers scene. His aspiration toward the pure and his abstraction toward the abyss will be a dominant image-symbol, commonly shared in European poetry.[5]

As part of his legacy to symbolism, Baudelaire communicated to posterity his two great literary predilections: Poe and Wagner—the one for his decadence, the other for his discovery of new combinations of artistic communication. Both were to be further explored by the Symbolist coterie which, under the guidance of Mallarmé, was to adopt Poe as one of its patrons and

5 Cf. Helen Bailey, *Hamlet in France from Voltaire to Laforgue* (Geneva: Droz, 1964).

was to call one of its most important journals *La Revue Wagnerienne.*

We shall see how the symbolist ego, the symbolist cosmopolitanism, and the whole range of ambiguities of discourse will come to fruition from the seed that Baudelaire sowed so nonchalantly and unwittingly.

IV

VERLAINE,
NOT RIMBAUD

For reasons that were tragic, the names of Verlaine and Rimbaud have been coupled in the annals of literary history, particularly in connection with the development of poetic theory revolving around the notion of symbolism. The critic Albert Thibaudet, who has done much to clarify the intricacies of the Symbolist school of the 1880's, has in respect to Rimbaud helped to perpetuate an erroneous impression. In his famed article "Révolution des Cinq" and in his study *Le Triptyque de la poésie moderne: Verlaine, Rimbaud, Mallarmé,* he joins these three poets as the founders of a poetic revolution culminating in the Symbolist movement. He tells us that Symbolism became aware in 1884–86 of "a revolution which took place fifteen years earlier with Rimbaud, Verlaine, Mallarmé, Lautréamont, Corbière." [1] This implies a relationship of thought, an alliance of purpose, an awareness of a uniform aesthetics by the five mentioned. If we are to distinguish symbolism from other trends and waves that emerged from the same literary ambience, we have to proceed, as the scientist, to isolate one element from among heterogeneous ones.

In this process of elimination, starting from the most obvious, we can immediately discount Lautréamont

[1] Albert Thibaudet, "Révolution des Cinq," Revue de Paris (15 août, 1934), p. 772.

and Corbière as far as their contribution to the literary school of the 1880's is concerned or their influence on the changes that occurred at that time in poetic concepts. Both young poets, in different ways non-traditional in their writings, were first published in the early 1870's and quickly went out of print, to remain unknown until the end of the century. Lautréamont, in fact, failed to gain any kind of reputation until the 1920's, when the surrealists hailed him as one of their literary saints, and new editions, illustrated by such as Dali and Valentine Hugo, took him out of his nineteenth-century frame and made him a twentieth-century poet. Corbière, like Rimbaud, came into personal, rather than literary prominence because he was mentioned in that famed work of biographical criticism which Verlaine called *Les Poètes maudits* (1884), a book that was widely read in the 1880's; it was by reading this book that T. S. Eliot later came to know of Corbière and contributed much in the early 1900's to Corbière's belated fame. Because Eliot coupled Corbière's name with that of Jules Laforgue, whose writings had appeared when the Symbolist school was at its peak and are therefore closely associated with the movement, Corbière's work has been accepted as part of the Symbolist heritage by Eliot's contemporaries and essentially on his say-so. For the French Symbolists, Corbière was a name only, certainly not an agent in the formulation of their poetic theories. Nor was he even an unwitting symbolist, as in some respects Baudelaire appears to have been.

As a matter of fact, the broad statement we have quoted about the five poets appears in another context in a more limited form, as Thibaudet signals and defines the notion of "triptych," saying: "after 1885 we have before us . . . a school which grows for a number of years in the face of public astonishment and derision but which will gradually dominate, renew French poetry, and of which Verlaine, Mallarmé, and Rimbaud will remain the three dominant names." [2]

What Rimbaud, Verlaine, and Mallarmé have in common is the fact that they produced their major works at about the same time, in the early 1870's, although Mallarmé's principal poems had already been worked out in the latter part of the 1860's. The character of the works of these three poets remains quite different; if it is true that Verlaine and Mallarmé are directly related to the Symbolist school, each in his distinctive fashion, Rimbaud's name belongs in the Symbolist ranks by personal association only. One might say that he is a member of the Symbolist family as an "in-law," through his personal relationships with Verlaine.

The fact that Rimbaud was a greater innovator than any of the Symbolists has nothing to do with the fact that he is not really in their orbit. His inclusion among the ranks of the precursors of symbolism has simply complicated the history of the Symbolist movement, bringing many a critic to the conclusion that Symbolism is heterogeneous, or at least a wavering between two contradictory commitments. Such is Edmund Wilson's attitude when he confronts Axël, the hero of Villiers, with the adventurer Rimbaud, suggesting two alternative forms of the Symbolist ideal: withdrawal into inaction and the dream, or flight into reality away from literature. But Rimbaud was in reality the only one who chose the so-called "escape from literature." If Rimbaud, and his purely personal adventure, is withdrawn from the Symbolist picture, the focus becomes much clearer, the ideals more uniform, the concepts less conflicting, the movement and its long-range development far more homogeneous.

2 Albert Thibaudet, *Le Triptyque de la poésie moderne: Verlaine, Rimbaud, Mallarmé. (Causeries Françaises,* 2e Année, 2e causerie, supplément à la Bibliothèque de la France no. 7 du 15 février 1924), p. 25.

In determining why Rimbaud is not a symbolist either in the broad sense or in the French (literal) sense of the word, we shall be defining at the same time what the far-reaching characteristics of symbolism are, and aiming at an evaluation of its heritage.

Rimbaud, like Baudelaire before him, like Verlaine and many others of his time, and like poets who were quite different in character (such as Gautier, Lautréamont, Banville, as well as others who today have no prominence in literary history), had felt that the direct discourse of the Romanticists, which had been the mode of communication, was no longer tolerable. The particularly subjective style of Alfred de Musset, who was the prototype of the French Romantic poet, was a special target of criticism. The desire for a more indirect form of verbal communication was a literary aim shared by many mid-century writers, and it cannot be attributed exclusively to the symbolist lineage. The symbolists were to achieve a distinct type of indirect discourse, of which we have seen traces in Baudelaire and which will evolve into a new technique during the latter part of the century.

The now famous letter of May 15, 1871, that Rimbaud wrote as a youth of seventeen to Paul Demeny attacks this problem: "So many *egotists* proclaim themselves authors!" [3] he exclaims, and then proceeds to show that the notion of the ego is in need of revision. The more subtle and profound cult of the ego suggested by Rimbaud revised the poetic notion of the unconscious and of the dream state for future poets, but it had no direct bearing on the Symbolists of the 1880's. This was for the quite simple reason that the Rimbaud letter did not appear in print until 1912— in time to serve as a manifesto for the surrealists. There are also evidences of the cosmopolitanism and the dis-

[3] The works of Rimbaud quoted in this chapter are from Rimbaud, *Oeuvres complètes* (Paris: Bibliothèque de la Pléiade, 1957).

tinction between things Parisian and things French
that we have already noted in Baudelaire—but again
all this could not have had any influence on the Symbolists. Rimbaud agrees with Baudelaire that the poet
has to be a seer, a visionary; he reiterates Baudelaire's
desire for a quest of *the new*. He welcomes the poetic
possibilities that are inherent in the disturbance and
turbulence of the senses that Baudelaire had described
in his accounts of hashish, and he goes one step further
by suggesting that the poet, in cultivating his inner
resources, must *consciously* disturb his senses.

The letter seems to have been written after a feverish
reading of Baudelaire. At the impressionable age of
seventeen, Rimbaud captured the essence of a variety
of pronouncements; with Baudelaire's notions of Swedenborgism, for example, he fused those of Fourier
and of other illuminists who dreamed of a universal
language. But if there was an affinity between Baudelaire and Rimbaud, their shared tendencies were to
come to the Symbolists through Baudelaire and not
through Rimbaud's more concise postulates. Had Rimbaud's letter been printed when it was written, had
Rimbaud lived in Paris and continued not only to
make pronouncements but to produce in accordance
with his theories, then Symbolism might never have
flourished, and surrealism might have had an earlier
start. On the other hand, had Rimbaud only written
what he did write and no more, had he not had the
publicity that came to him because of his relationship
with Verlaine, his case would have been similar to
Lautréamont's—his reputation delayed to a later epoch
—and he would not have become a confusing factor in
the history of symbolism.

As it is, in appraising the character and the values
of the heritage of symbolism, we have to survey symbolism from the vantage point of the Symbolists and
recognize how different Rimbaud's work was from the
rest of the poetry published during the same years

under the Symbolist aegis. "Voyelles" and "Le Bateau ivre" appeared in the early 1880's; *Une Saison en enfer,* which had appeared in a small edition in Belgium, did not really get much distribution, except among Rimbaud's friends, until Verlaine brought out a definitive edition of all of Rimbaud's major writings in 1892. Most of *Les Illuminations,* which is the major reason for Rimbaud's eminent position among poets today, was published in 1886 in the Symbolist review *La Vogue,* under the direction of Gustave Kahn, the Symbolist theoretician. Although the controversy over dates is not yet resolved—whether *Les Illuminations* was written before or after *Une Saison en enfer*—the years are those very important ones between 1870 and 1875, in which Mallarmé's major poems were being completed or revised, in which Lautréamont had written his single work and perished, in which Verlaine's most symbolist collection of verse, *Romances sans paroles,* had been published.

Without *Les Illuminations,* it is doubtful that Rimbaud would have the major stature he has today; yet this collection comes on the literary horizon suddenly in 1886, after staying in Charles Sivry's pocket for some seven years. Whatever theories the Symbolists were to develop and substantiate have already been shaped, as have the minds of the numerous poets who call themselves "Symbolists." While they are in the process of forming their poetic techniques, they have been exposed to Verlaine's *Romances sans paroles* and to the personal influence of Mallarmé in his salon of the Rue de Rome; they have heard his poems read in various stages of their development, even if these have not been widely disseminated, and know him well for his theories on language and the metaphor. But of Rimbaud they know his reputation as a child prodigy, his virtuosity, as demonstrated in that extraordinary feat of writing "Le Bateau ivre," the poem of voyage to end all voyages, anti-Romantic in character rather

than *pro* any new form. They know that Rimbaud
invented the colors of the vowels and produced rather
cleverly cryptic images associated with them; that, as
his farewell to literature, following his abysmal homo-
sexual adventure with his fellow-poet Verlaine, he
wrote a quasi-biographical prose poem of an amor-
phous nature in which he described the brutalities and
the mental aberrations connected with the passage
through inferno that occurs when life ceases to be the
festive dream of childhood, when the magic fades away,
when love becomes a deception and the God we have
been waiting for fails to appear. His stoical emergence
from the lonely spiritual battle for identification with
the human and the divine is a particularly excruciating
demonstration of the cult of the ego. But the art of
the boy genius remains uncomprehended not only in
his own time; as late as the 1920's there is no real attempt at analysis of his remarkable technique. The
chief interest in Rimbaud from Verlaine to Edmund
Wilson has been the poem of his life, the ill-fated
companionship with Verlaine, the flights from society,
the farewell to poetry, the life in Ethiopia, the pathetic
return and death from cancer of the leg, and, according to the testimony of his sister, the eventual conversion to Catholicism. When it was not his life, then it
was the sources of his poetry that attracted the critics;
his role in the ambience of the *Coin de Table,* where
one day he drank absinthe with a group of pre-Symbol-
ists before he rejected Paris, as he had earlier rejected
the provinces.

The truth of the matter is that Rimbaud's writing
employs many Romantic devices, including the in-
sufferable "I" in *Une Saison en enfer.* It also becomes
more and more apparent that the radical departure
from the rest of his writing which *Les Illuminations*
reveals is not recognized by his contemporaries; and
there is not a single imitator of the poetic technique
he creates in *Les Illuminations* at any time during the

fin de siècle, either in France or abroad. Rimbaud was to that epoch another Chatterton and nothing more, a flash of lightning too swift and too bright to leave more than a dazzling but ephemeral impression behind.

Although *Romances sans paroles* and "Art poétique" (1874, printed 1882) spring out of the same years and are written practically side by side with *Les Illuminations,* in the most intimate personal relationship that could exist between two artists, they are not merely two sides of the same coin, they are as different as the coins of two separate countries. So much opportunity for cross-influence, yet so much difference of vision, of character, and of poetic communication! The destiny of two major aesthetic movements can be viewed in observing the distance between these two beings and their art.

It is a pity that of late it has become fashionable for those who consider the poems of Paul Verlaine to approach him under the influence of their infatuation with Rimbaud. The Pléiade edition of his complete works constantly reminds the reader that Verlaine is not Rimbaud; and what a pity, it implies, Rimbaud would have done this or that so much better! What seems to be forgotten is that Verlaine was a tremendously prolific poet who had a major influence on the poetry of Western Europe at the end of the nineteenth century and in the early years of the twentieth. In fact, in some European countries his influence, which has been synonymous with the influence of Symbolism, has not yet ceased. Comparing his numerous and universally communicable works with the dense, cryptic, hermetic writings of Rimbaud, limited in volume and profound in implications, writings whose influence is in ascendance today, although their comprehensive availability and dissemination are more difficult, is like comparing, in an earlier period, the gigantic output of Victor Hugo with the small but lush harvest of Baudelaire. If such comparisons are made to show diverse facets of the human temperament and of trends in art, the analysis can be beneficial; but to depreciate the quality of the one in boosting the value of the other leads to the comprehension of neither one. The work of Verlaine has yet to find its definitive critic.

Both *Les Illuminations* and *Romances sans paroles* consist of a series of kaleidoscopes in which the outer landscape provides the target for the inner mood. In both cases there is the will not to communicate the subjective state directly to the reader, but to veil the purely biographical by means of metaphoric devices. There the similarity ends, although strangely enough much of the exterior décor is the same: the countryside of Belgium and England. Each poet appropriated the scenery in his own fashion.

Verlaine had already practiced the art of suggestive writing in *Fêtes galantes;* he had already linked the landscape of the soul with the man-made tapestries of a Watteau scene and shown how much more subtle is the bittersweet of emotions than either the sweet or the bitter.

CLAIR DE LUNE

Votre âme est un paysage choisi
Que vont charmant masques et bergamasques,
Jouant du luth et dansant et quasi
Tristes sous leurs déguisements fantasques.

Tout en chantant sur le mode mineur
L'amour vainqueur et la vie opportune,
Ils n'ont pas l'air de croire à leur bonheur
Et leur chanson se mêle au clair de lune,

Au calme clair de lune triste et beau,
Qui fait rêver les oiseaux dans les arbres
Et sangloter d'extase les jets d'eau,
Les grands jets d'eau sveltes parmi les marbres.[4]

4 The quotations from the works of Verlaine used in this chapter are from Verlaine, *Oeuvres complètes* (Paris: Bibliothèque de la Pléiade, 1957).

MOONLIGHT

Your soul is an exquisite landscape
That bergamasks have charmed. Enchanting bands
Playing the lute and dancing to escape
The sadness left untouched by mummers' hands.

Chanting the while upon the minor mode
Of happy love and of life's long delight
Shyly they tread upon the happy road
And their sweet music sighs in the moonlight.

In sad moonlight, serene in its beauty,
Birds cease their song and dream under its spell;
And graceful waters sob in ecstasy
Surging from the marbles in which they dwell.

In suggesting the characteristic quality of the beloved, Verlaine says that her soul is a landscape where
they sing of gay things in minor keys. He had also discovered in the same volume that the half-light is richer
in suggestive power and for stimulating the imagination than the bright sunlight, and that words which
imply emotion are more powerful in communicating
that emotion than words which designate it. These
discoveries come into greater fulfillment in *Romances
sans paroles,* where the slices of scenery act as a prism
between the poet's delicate sensitivity and the reader's
receptivity. With the simplest words in the French language (it is not surprising that he has been so readily
translated into many languages!) he sets moods, as a
musician sets a key: skies, clouds, the moon, the wind,
the snow, the crows, rain, the plain—these nouns, so
often used by Verlaine, were to become in symbolist
vocabulary recognizable, unfortunately too recognizable, as symbols, losing eventually what concrete attributes they may have retained in Verlaine's poetry.
They were to be coupled with the most non-specific
adjectives possible—grey, pale, uncertain, white, placid,
deep, fleeting, soft—and with verbs suggestive of melan-

choly rather than of passion—such as to cry, to whim-
per, to be bored, to blow, to sigh, to tremble, to flee—
sounds as muted as the grey of skies, as the sound of
water on moss.

The stage is indeed set for symbolist imagery. Poetry
is music, as he will repeat in his famous line of "Art
poétique": "De la musique avant toute chose," and
it is often obvious that in his choice of words his first
concern is for the sound of the phrase rather than for
the sense that it conveys. He was also to say in "Art
poétique" that the poet must seek irregularity of metrical form; yet in reality his works demonstrate less of
this range of poetic instrumentalization than those of
his successors, such as René Ghil and the *vers libristes*.
His poetry is a veritable demonstration of the music
of words, but not as Baudelaire had understood the
music of poetry to be the power of music inherent in
words.

It is to be noted that there are, in effect, three differing concepts of music in nineteenth-century poetry.
The first, as seen in Baudelaire, finds in words the same
suggestive properties that are inherent in musical notes:
evocative of mood, but without communicating specific meaning. In Verlaine's poetry, it is not the single
word that sets in motion associations of images in the
reader's mind, or stirs vague emotions, as does music;
instead, the associations of special combinations of
words, containing such recurrences of sounds as "il
pleure dans mon coeur," sound in effect like music.
They make music in the same way as the harmony of
a series of musical sounds. Poetry becomes music
through its appeal to the ear rather than in its inherent
function or in its effect on mental associations. A third
quality of music in poetry was to be demonstrated by
Mallarmé, who was to simulate the very composition
of the musical work: theme and variations, symphonic
orchestration of phrasing, the pauses—white spaces—
between images as between notes, the verbal image

replacing the musical phrase, a form underlying poems as diverse as "L'Après-midi d'un faune" and "Un Coup de dés jamais n'abolira le hasard." Although the manner of Baudelaire and that of Mallarmé were far more subtle and challenging to the intelligence of the creative artist, it must be admitted that the more simple and more lyrical manner of Verlaine was to have the greatest effect on symbolist technique both in France and Spain and in middle Europe.

Finally, here and there in his *chanson grise,* Verlaine conveyed the taste of death, the tremor of the ephemeral, the smell of the decaying as it permeated his fragile scene. He pronounced the word "mourir" with a rapture of satiation and fulfillment. In this sense, he added a few more strokes to the portrait of the "decadent" and the spirit of decadence that we have already vaguely discerned in Baudelaire. In defining it, he said: "I like the word 'decadence' with its reflections of purple and gold." This word suggested the refined thoughts of the extremely civilized man, possessed of delicate senses, a soul capable of intensive pleasures (*voluptés*). Decadence is "the art of dying in beauty." In speaking of Verlaine, the critic Jacques Rivière said, in 1906: "He was unconscious of the value of what he was doing. . . . We are now used to a poetry that finds the unconscious state only through a great deal of conscious effort. Symbolism in this sense is the opposite of Verlaine." [5] The statement is ambivalent. It is true that Verlaine is a spontaneous writer, from whom poetry poured forth as song poured from the pen of Schubert. What he codified in "Art poétique" is no doubt an *a posteriori* theory, summarizing what he had previously achieved rather than preparing the ground for future work. This is borne out by the fact that *Sagesse,* his subsequent work, and his later poetry is much less Symbolist in technique than those

[5] Jacques Rivière, *Correspondance: Jacques Rivière et Alain Fournier,* Vol. II (Paris: NRF, 10 août, 1906), p. 192.

of his works that date from the 1870's. But this spontaneity is equally germane to much of the Symbolist poetry of the 1880's. The true Symbolist poet was prolific in all countries; he wrote with facility, and his inspiration was abundant as it rose out of the very rapture of the words he used and delighted in.

Only Rimbaud and Mallarmé were in this sense deliberate poets, miserly of their words and quite conscious of the uses to which they were putting their innermost sensations. But it is this very difference that separates them from the Symbolist norm. Symbolism does not find its opposite in Verlaine; it is Rimbaud as poet and Mallarmé as theoretician who are the opposites of Symbolism. It is true that in his early short poems Rimbaud caught the magnetism in words that draw sound and meaning together into an hypnotic musicality:

O saisons, ô châteaux,
Quelle âme est sans défauts?

O saisons, ô châteaux,

J'ai fait la magique étude
Du bonheur, que nul n'élude.

O vive lui, chaque fois
Que chante le coq gaulois.

Mais je n'aurai plus d'envie,
Il s'est chargé de ma vie.

Ce charme! il prit âme et corps,
Et dispersa tous efforts.

Que comprendre à ma parole?
Il fait qu'elle fuie et vole!

O saisons, ô châteaux!

This poetic technique should have made Rimbaud only a secondary figure of symbolism. But in the cluster of prose poems that have come down to us as *Les Illu-*

minations and which are the basis for his great poetic stature, Rimbaud deviates from the manner of Verlaine on every score. His notion of suggestive rather than direct discourse is quite different from Verlaine's. Whereas Verlaine seeks the infinite possibilities of the vague and the uncertainties of nuance, Rimbaud provides in his landscapes stark, concrete details—disconnected yet juxtaposed, so as to remain even more tantalizingly ambiguous than vague language. This is true even when he is conveying biographical experiences. The incomplete is as obscure in meaning as the vague; concretely descriptive adjectives designating colors can be as mysterious, when their associations are not logically or graphically demonstrated, as vaporous, abstract, non-descriptive images. With this concrete but occult language Rimbaud invents new flowers, for example:

FLEURS

D'un gradin d'or,—parmi les cordons de soie, les gazes grises, les velours verts et les disques de cristal qui noircissent comme du bonze au soleil,—je vois la digitale s'ouvrir sur un tapis de filigranes d'argent, d'yeux et de chevelures.

Des pièces d'or jaune semées sur l'agate, des piliers d'acajou supportant un dôme d'émeraudes, des bouquets de satin blanc et de fines verges de rubis entourent la rose d'eau.

Tels qu'un dieu aux énormes yeux bleus et aux formes de neige, la mer et le ciel attirent aux terrasses de marbre la foule des jeunes et fortes roses.

But the Symbolists of the 1880's were to adhere to the manner of Verlaine, to which they had been exposed for some ten years, rather than to that of Rimbaud, which had fallen like a meteor into sudden view in the mid-1880's. The sotto voce suggestiveness of Verlaine's images conveyed a sense of *intimacy;* the naked fragments communicated by Rimbaud were to give him an almost total *privacy* of meaning, which to this day his commentators are trying indefatigably to break through. Verlaine won out, for intimacy was to be the dominant tone of the Symbolists.

Where Verlaine seeks to veil nature, Rimbaud talks of unveiling or illuminating it, and of finding its primeval colors. Chidingly, he recounts in "Vagabonds" how he had tried to restore his companion to his primordial status of son of the sun, but he implies that he failed to move the nocturnal creature that Verlaine was to a place in the sun. Again, the Symbolists, following in Verlaine's rather than Rimbaud's footsteps, will choose the moon as their light, rather than the sun. Whereas Verlaine, as he describes himself, is the super-civilized man of the end of the century, Rimbaud is antediluvian in his visions, exploring the genesis of his sensations rather than their waning apotheosis, such as was to be the case with the Symbolists who followed swooning in Verlaine's path.

Much as Rimbaud admired Baudelaire, he accused him of having frequented the artistic milieus too much; Verlaine also is the indoor aesthete; and so will be all the other Symbolists. Rimbaud is the man on the road, the great walker, who strides across the length and breadth of Europe. He is the outdoor man, in sharp contrast to the Symbolist who encloses himself in paludal, airtight chambers, behind shuttered, darkened windows. He seeks bright dawns instead of twilights; he does not retreat into dark interiors, even in the midst of his spiritual crisis. Instead, as the last page of his metaphysical diary, *Une Saison en enfer,* suggests: "Let us receive all the influxes of vigor and real tenderness. And at daybreak, armed with an ardent patience, we shall enter into the splendid cities."

The vocabulary employed by the two poets is extraordinarily different. It is hard to imagine what Arthur Symons, the English author of *The Symbolist Movement,* meant when he said that Rimbaud was abstract. Perhaps he meant that the images were difficult for the usual imagination to visualize. Actually, Rimbaud's vocabulary is one of the most concrete in the French language, after that of Villon and Rabelais. Where Verlaine's vocabulary is simple and generalized, Rimbaud uses words that are rare and particularized, the multiplicity of meaning rising out of the variety of their uses rather than out of the vagueness of meaning, a trick that Mallarmé will also perform in the second stage of his writing and which will go unnoticed until well into the twentieth century.

If there is musicality in Rimbaud's words, particularly in his verse passages, the musical attributes of the words are of secondary importance to their visual qualities. Priority is given to the visual, rather than to the musical appeal. Again in this respect Rimbaud seems to have foreshadowed the affinity between poetry and art which was to develop in the twentieth century, rather than the more immediate link with music that was to occur within his own era. Nor did Rimbaud consciously experiment with freedom of versification. Curiously, along with Lautréamont, he went in one leap from verse to cadenced prose, thereby implying that the true character of poetry does not lie in its exterior form, but depends on the mental process.

Finally, the decadence of Rimbaud is not at all of the nature of the Symbolist "decadence" that we have sought to define. If there is indeed decadence in the delinquent youth who took Verlaine away from his family, who scorned his own kin and lived a most irregular life, this is not the notion of "decadence" that is significant within the context of Symbolism. His decadence has a moral connotation, stemming from infraction of society's rules; what we have seen in the case of Baudelaire, however, and will see later in Villiers, Hofmannsthal, Rilke, D'Annunzio—i.e. "decadence" in its symbolist sense—is the state of mind of the poet who is haunted by the cruelty of Father Time and the imminence of death. It is an engrossment with self and with the mysteries of an inner fixation on the incomprehensible limits of life and death; it is the delicacies of the oversensitive.

Rimbaud does not talk of death, or feel its presence, or swoon in terror of it. The theme of death, which was to become one of the basic subjects whereby symbolism is recognizable in poetry, as well as in the drama, is totally absent from Rimbaud's work. Even his Hell in *Une Saison en enfer* is not an imaginative conception of an after-death, but a delirium here on earth. His metaphysics has the concrete reality of physical hallucination, rather than the rarefied atmosphere of the void, so eloquently represented by the symbolists. And he does not live long enough, nor even sit still long enough, to experience the *ennui,* the fundamental *angst* of the symbolist fraternity. He is a force, a gust of wind, that leaves havoc behind him, and is better known by the effect he has had on those who saw him go by than by what they remember of his presence.

From this confrontation of Verlaine and Rimbaud, Verlaine emerges as the "great poet," as the Englishman George Moore asserts in his *Confessions of a Young Man.* If "greatness" is judged by the degree of imitation a writer attracts, Verlaine is indeed the master; the variations on his themes and his style will multiply, generation after generation. While Mallarmé becomes the person one listens to, Verlaine is the one whose example as poet is more available and emulated. In his famous letter, speaking of the influence of Musset, Rimbaud had said: "At seventeen, every college student . . . writes his own *Rolla.*" One could say that every poet of the 1880's, and right up to the 1920's, has tried his hand at being Verlaine. If Mallarmé is symbolism in theory, Verlaine is symbolism in practice. Verlaine supplied the form, the vocabulary, the themes, the major symbols, the specific sources of animism in nature; he set the mood of ennui and bittersweet melancholy; he suggested the need for an air of mystery in the poetic setting. His great default was his failure to supply depth beyond the obscurity—the absense of premonition and wonder on his part in connection with the mysteries that many of his words suggested but did not authenticate. He used "mourir" (to die) with a voluptuousness which makes one suspect that he did not feel the impact of the event, so much as the sound of the word. With the same words, and in the same settings, symbolists after him were to convey a greater *mystique,* a more anguished decadence, a more haunting melody. Deeper natures than his own were to sense the invisible forces that obsess and pursue man, and give far graver reasons for melancholy than a frivolous heart or a rainy sky. The gamut of symbolism lies between the imitators and those who were able to transcend the model which Verlaine drafted for the Symbolist Movement.

V

MALLARME AND
THE SYMBOLIST
CENACLE

Mallarmé is not a Symbolist in the coterie sense of
the word, but he more than anyone else is responsible
for having brought Symbolism into being. (Christ was
not a Christian, although he initiated what was to
become Christianity; Marx was not a Communist.)
When in 1891 the journalist Jules Huret asked
Mallarmé if he was the creator of a new movement,
Mallarmé declined the honor, saying that he was an
individualist and a solitary man, and that his only
merit was to have inquired into what was new among
the most recent writings. He passed the distinction of
being *chef d'école* on to Verlaine with this comment:
"the father, the real father of the young is Verlaine,
that magnificent Verlaine." [1]

Mallarmé was too independent to be willing to pay
the price of leadership. Although current Mallarmé
criticism is sensing this in its efforts to find something
other than symbolism in Mallarmé's writings, Mallarmé
is not outside of the orbit of the movement in the
same manner as Rimbaud. For Rimbaud tried to cor-
rect what he thought to be wrong with the poetry of

[1] The quotations from the works of Mallarmé used in this
chapter are from Mallarmé, *Oeuvres complètes* (Paris: Bibliothèque de la Pléiade, 1945). The Huret-Mallarmé interview appears in the collected works under the title "Sur l'Evolution
littéraire."

his time, in a way that was quite different from that of the future Symbolists' concepts and practices. Moreover, as is shown by the dates of his publications and his isolation from his contemporaries, it was not possible for him to exert an influence on the Symbolists. The case with Mallarmé is quite different. Although even older than Rimbaud in relation to the Symbolist generation, he is closely associated with the younger poets, and he clearly shows empathy with them. In his autobiographical letter to Verlaine, which was to supply material for Verlaine's volume *Hommes d'Aujourd'hui* in 1885, he explains that he was ten years ahead of his time and was therefore more compatible with the younger poets; but at the same time he disavows any conscious intent to give them a direction. It was a meeting of minds, he says, rather than a question of influence.

In effect, Mallarmé is not, historically speaking, a Symbolist. If it is true that his poems were for the most part published in the collection *Vers et Prose* in 1887, one of the summit years of Symbolist publications, he considered these poems to be fragments and almost apologetically called the volume an "album" rather than a unified book. The poems it contains had been written, or had been germinating, during the 1860's and early 1870's, and were thus contemporary with those of Verlaine and Rimbaud, rather than with those of the young Symbolists with whom he was publishing concurrently.[2] Born in 1842, Mallarmé belonged to the age

2 The place of Mallarmé in the symbolist movement is in large part a matter of focus. If Baudelaire is considered a symbolist, then indeed Mallarmé would be in Sir Bowra's words: "the conclusion and crown of the Symbolist Movement," and after him everything would be anti-climatic. But if we are more interested in tracing the path of Symbolism in European poetry and the degree of viability manifested by symbolist aesthetics which were formulated not in 1857 but in 1886, the vantage point is shifted and Mallarmé does not loom as a summit, striking but barren; he becomes a fountainhead rich in sustenance, contributing to the richness of the poetic terrain.

group of Verlaine, Swinburne, George Moore, of such Parnassian contemporaries as Catulle Mendès and Théodore de Banville, and of that uncategorizable Villiers de l'Isle-Adam with whom he shared so many qualities, as well as of the artist Edouard Manet, whom he saw every day for ten years and who illustrated his most famous poem, "L'Après-midi d'un faune." These were his friends, who had long been exchanging ideas and works with him. But the poets who were to attend his famous Tuesday evening gatherings between 1882 and 1894 were not ten years, but closer to twenty years his juniors. When he became for them a teacher, a mentor, a sage, his own evolution was already complete, and his poetic vision in large part fixed.

Very often the work of Mallarmé is represented in a three-stage cycle: the classic; the mystic or dreamer; the hermetic or occult writer. Actually, as far as his poetic work is concerned, the three phases are almost simultaneous. Mallarmé was such a severe taskmaster, so hard on himself, and he probed his own mettle so deeply, that he was not able to produce more than a dozen great poems in his lifetime; in every case, a conflict arose between his love of the poem and the critical spirit that destroyed it while he was creating it. As a result, he spent his entire life working on his meager harvest of poetic survivals, polishing and repolishing them, and dreaming of the Great Work which was never to be written because the plane of perfection on which he placed it in his imagination forbade the possibility of its ever becoming a reality. When he could not find fulfillment in the creation of the perfect work, he transferred his aspirations to the discussion of poetry before the sympathetic audience he had gathered around him.

Mallarmé's poetic concerns were crystallized early in his life, when he sketched the forms they were to take; thereafter, he spent his life refining his attitudes and his forms. He was largely haunted by "ennui," by the "gouffre," its counterpart of "azur," and by the isolated status of the poet in society. These broad thematic lines are the closest he ever got to "subject matter," and his poems, long and short, reflected (proceeding from the "je" to the exterior world), or projected (creating an emblematic character), these intertwined preoccupations of the poet.

No one has ever expressed the "ennui" so briefly and so totally as he did in one of his early poems, "Brise marine": "La chair est triste, hélas! et j'ai lu tous les livres." In one alexandrine he ran the gamut of that boredom that neither the pleasures of the flesh nor those of the intellect can decrease. This weariness of the superrefined man and the impossibility of relief is one of the themes that Mallarmé was to use over and over again without ever being quite as subjective as the "je" in that line. He will cast as symbols of "ennui" mythological figures to which he will give his own particular meaning, in the two great poems, "Hérodiade" and "L'Après-midi d'un faune," that were conceived almost simultaneously and remained in his thoughts and under his pen for most of his career as a poet.

In "L'Après-midi d'un faune," Pan, who is generally identified as a sensualist, takes on an intellectualized sensualism as a release from physical sensuality, seeking escape in his inner images of ideal sexual pleasure, which loom more powerful than actual physical eroticism:

> je vais parler longtemps
> Des déesses; et par d'idolâtres peintures,
> A leur ombre enlever encore des ceintures:

As he holds up the grape that has become hollow and unappetizing, he juxtaposes to its emptiness the teeming memory:

O nymphes, regonflons des SOUVENIRS divers.

In presenting the paradox of the deflated symbol of sensuality and its infusion with the breath of memory and dreams, Mallarmé implies that inner sensuality, by its intensity and boldness, can compensate for the futile and fleeting character of physical experience. The Symbolists will seek this same kind of refuge from overt and tedious reality. Those verses of Mallarmé's poem in which memory and dream appear more powerfully sensual than actual experience, place him most in line with Symbolism. It is significant to note that they are the center of an illuminating article by L. J. Austin, in which he compares the three versions of "L'Après-midi d'un faune" and, computing the lexicography, arrives at the objective discovery that these lines remain basically intact as the poem undergoes change after change. Professor Austin concludes that, in their constancy amid the variants, they constitute in fact the nucleus of the poem and become symbolic of "un principe essentiel de l'esthétique mallarméen: celui de la 'divine transposition' qui 'va du fait à l'idéal'." [3]

But even as he wrote "L'Après-midi d'un faune" Mallarmé had already seen the other side of the coin: satiation with the dream. Escape is not a simple matter for a complicated man like Mallarmé. If one horn of his dilemma is evidenced by the Faun, the other is symbolized by Hérodiade. Mallarmé's composite nature envisages flight *from* flight, as the "ennui" persists unrelieved. Hérodiade is the image of saturated introspection; that is how her Nurse describes her before she makes her entry:

3 Cf. L. J. Austin, " 'L'Après-midi d'un faune,' de Stéphane Mallarmé: lexiques comparés des trois états du poème," *Studi in Onore di Carlo Pellegrini*, Biblioteca di "Studi Francesi," II (1963), 733–38. Professor Austin sees in Mallarmé's powerful evocation of memory a path that leads straight to Proust, who proved for all time that time lost can indeed become time recovered and is thereby more vital than it was in its original form.

l'enfant, exilée en son coeur précieux
Comme un cygne cachant en sa plume ses yeux,

She is indeed tired of the escape that others seek when
they are tired of reality. She has discovered the hollow-
ness of dreams as she has contemplated the sterile
mirror which reflects the futility of her inner life:

O miroir!
Eau froide par l'ennui dans ton cadre gelée
Que de fois et pendant des heures, désolée
Des songes et cherchant mes souvenirs qui sont
Comme des feuilles sous ta glace au trou profond,
Je m'apparus en toi comme une ombre lointaine,
Mais, horreur! des soirs, dans ta sévère fontaine,
J'ai de mon rêve épars connu la nudité!

She emerges, then, for a brief encounter with reality as
she projects her timid soul into the chamber, into contact with another human being, the Nurse, who is
waiting for her there. Cruelly, the Nurse points out to
her that the solitude within which she has enveloped
herself harbors only a "vain mystery." But Hérodiade's
exposure to reality is even more fleeting than are the
dreams of Pan. After a futile moment of waiting for she
knows not what, she withdraws quickly into her in-
activity and purity, which are symptomatic of her inherent and unsurmountable fear of getting hurt by life.

"Hérodiade," as the counterpart of "L'Après-midi
d'un faune," will be as significant in setting a Symbolist
attitude as the obsessive narcissism, unrewarding as it
is exitless, becomes one of the salient motives of the
"decadent" spirit, accentuating a fear of love and sexu-
ality but also the failure of spiritual substitutes. Of
this we shall see striking examples in Laforgue and
Villiers de l'Isle-Adam, and in the theater of the *fin de
siècle.*

Mallarmé's ambivalence prevails in his confronta-

tion with the "gouffre," as it does with "ennui." No
doubt he first became obsessed with the equivocal character of the abyss, as a pit and as a gateway to man's
imagination, through his reading of Baudelaire, which
was one of the great literary experiences of his early
youth. Here again the image has two facets as it indicates the black chaos of nothingness and the blue totality beyond the visible limits of the earth. In two
early poems, "Les Fenêtres" and "L'Azur," we witness
two aspects of the attraction. In "Les Fenêtres" he sees
himself with featherless wings, unable to make the leap
from reality: "Ici-bas est maître," despite all effort and
desire; but in "L'Azur," although now revolt from
reality seems futile to him, by a strange perversity, the
"Azur" calls him more urgently than before, in what
is almost a traumatic compulsion:

En vain! l'Azur triomphe, et je l'entends qui chante
Dans les cloches. Mon âme, il se fait voix pour plus
Nous faire peur avec sa victoire méchante,
Et du métal vivant sort en bleus angélus!

Il roule par la brume, ancien et traverse
Ta native agonie, ainsi qu'un glaive sûr;
Où fuir dans la révolte inutile et perverse?
Je suis hanté. L'Azur! l'Azur! l'Azur! l'Azur!

"Azur," a word untranslatable into English, but com-
bining the meanings of "blue" and "sky" and its mysterious impermeability, will become one of the literary
conventions of symbolism: when the Latin American
poet Rubén Darío calls his first significant volume of
verse *Azul*, the Spanish word assumes the metaphysical
meaning that Mallarmé had given to its French equivalent. Thereafter, the word becomes part of the symbolist code, as linguistically universal as it is conceptu-
ally complex.

Twice in his literary career Mallarmé attempted to
probe the darker side of "azur," i.e. the "gouffre," but
each time he came away with a sense of the futility of

the quest, and of the devastating impotence of man's metaphysical ventures. The first was the descent into man's own being, which he attempted in the prose poem "Igitur"; the second, a verbal venture into outer space. The result of the first voyage was a simulation of personal death; the second left him and the reader with a sense of cosmic disintegration. The first work was conceived too early and published too late to have affected Symbolism. "Un Coup de dés jamais n'abolira le hasard" was completed at the end of his life and not published until the end of the century; it was not able, therefore, to influence the ideas nor the techniques of the Symbolist *cénacle*.

These poems throw more light on Mallarmé than on symbolism; but comparing the early work with the later one on more or less the same theme, one can discern that during his lifetime, having associated with the Symbolist writers and preached to them the theory of the purification of the Word—"donner un sens plus purs aux mots de la tribu," as he put it in his "Le Tombeau d'Edgar Poe"—he had himself purified his own language, distilled the image to the point of spiritualizing even the use of concrete words, found a vocabulary for purely abstract poetry. "Un Coup de dés" is virtually an anti-poem; it is written not in free verse but in a fragmentation of verse that reduces the earth and its Orphic meaning almost to an algebraic formula. If we were to discuss these two poems in detail, we would deviate from the mainstream of symbolism, for nothing in the symbolist tradition was to be so obscure, so remote from ordinary communication as were these two poems. It is only in terms of Mallarmé's concept of music, the affinities between music and poetry, that "Un Coup de dés" is important to the comprehension of symbolism, and then only, as we shall see later on, as a negation of Symbolism's concepts of musical composition and of the Symbolists' verbal simulations of it.

If not through contact with these two poems, then surely through their contact with the man who wrote them, the Symbolists were to be imbued with the notion that the foremost mission of the poet, particularly in a materialistic age, is to recapture the sense of the mystery of existence. Mallarmé said to them: "Whatever is sacred, whatever remains sacred, must be clothed in mystery." [4] As for the isolation of the poet, Mallarmé took an unequivocal stand on that subject, which he conveyed to his followers. He felt that, in a society that made no official place for, nor gave any recognized rank to the poet, the poet did not need to concern himself with society. He had the right to withdraw from the circle of social action, to work in solitary or in sheltered surroundings, and once in a while to send a poem—a visiting card, as it were—to the world, to remind it of his existence. Most of the Symbolists were to acquiesce in this attitude and to go out of their way to create a gulf between themselves and the public; they drew closer to each other in order to remain the more withdrawn from the world. The ivory tower became in truth a reality, a symbol of the poet's stand, a sharp reversal of the attitude of Victor Hugo or Tennyson, who had thought of themselves as the eloquent spokesmen of the people, the voice of humanity.

Mallarmé was drawn to the image of Hamlet as the symbol of the nonparticipant, whose sensibility and power to dream ran counter to the mediocrity of existence. He identified with this image, and thereafter there is a veritable cult of Hamlet, not only as the solitary hero, but for his taste for the macabre. There is indeed a dissociation for the Symbolists between Hamlet and Shakespeare, as the human problems of the Hamlet in Shakespeare's play are minimized by the Symbolists, and the legendary character of the Nordic Narcissus, with his intellectual vagaries and morbidi-

---

4 Mallarmé, "Autobiographie," *op. cit.*, p. 664.

ties, becomes the symbol of the prevailing mood.

Unwittingly, Mallarmé was proving himself a "decadent" in the symbolist sense of the word, although certainly not in the moral sense, for a more proper, ethical literary man would be hard to find. He himself disliked the word "decadent"; as he said to Verlaine, who was using the title "Décadence": "What an abominable title is *Décadence;* it is high time to get rid of everything that resembles it!" [5] He also protested against a notorious book by Max Nordau entitled *Dégénerescence,* in which he saw a confusion of the meanings of degeneration and hypersensitivity. Nonetheless, he himself was a "decadent" in that sense in which we have been considering the word from the beginning of this study—the "decadent" spirit without which the purely technical changes that symbolism brought to prosody would have no great significance. The word "fall," which Mallarmé says he loves, is identified with the agonizing pleasure of the poetry of the dying Roman Empire. He implies the convergence of a historical and mystical state, which later emerges in Yeats as the image of Byzantium.

In Mallarmé's writings, as well as in his personal behavior, this "decadence," as we have seen is apparent in the overpowering "ennui" of his existence, translated into objects and projected upon characters, his preoccupation with the imponderable "gouffre" or "azur," the futility of thought that will be swallowed up in death, the impossibility of escape from the sense of temporality, the acute sensitivity, the tendency to reduce life to inaction and the dream, the withdrawal from the mainstream, the cloistered look, the Hamlet gesture, the notation of the fluctuations of human whims. Mallarmé, indeed, set the tone for this "decadence" of the waning years of the nineteenth century.

"Symbolist and Decadent!" Too often histories of

---

[5] Mallarmé, "Notes et Variantes," *ibid.,* p. 1444.

literature suggest that the famous "and" is really an "or." But the "and" is truer than the "or," and any suggestion of a duality is in truth a fallacy. The one could not exist without the other, and Mallarmé proved it from the very start by his own existence, in his writings as in his conversations, although he would not have applied either label to himself. What prevents the "decadent" from becoming a neurasthenic, a pathological figure—i.e., from truly identifying with Huysmans' fictional prototype, Des Esseintes—is that the "decadent" writer projects his attitude upon art; he directs the cult of his ego to an exterior symbol, which his highly creative mind is capable of transforming into a thing of beauty. "Where there is symbol, there is creation," said Mallarmé to Jules Huret in the much-quoted interview of 1891.

If then, in terms of the crystallization of the "decadent" spirit, Mallarmé had an effect upon Symbolism, how far did his own technique of poetic creation merge with the Symbolists' innovations? The comprehension of the relationship between Mallarmé's aesthetics and that of the Symbolists hinges first of all on an understanding of the meaning Mallarmé gives to "symbol." When he says to Jules Huret, "Where there is symbol, there is creation," his notion of symbol is more encompassing than the meaning that the Symbolist *cénacle* gave to the word. He seems to foresee both symbolist and surrealist techniques when he envisages the two faces of the poetic alchemy at the same time in that highly significant statement: "It is the perfect use of this mystery that constitutes symbol: to evoke an object, little by little, in order to show a mood or, conversely, to select an object and to extricate a mood from it, by means of a series of decodings." The object created in order to evoke a "mood" (*état d'âme*) was in line with the aspirations of the symbolists, whereas the opposite operation, inherent in the second part of the sentence, which consists of decipher-

ing an object or emblem of material reality into subjective interpretations gives premonitions of surrealism.

But what interests us here is the extent to which the
first operation coincides with the Symbolist conception
of poetry. In the expression "to evoke an object little
by little, in order to show a mood," it is the first part
of the sentence that generally provokes comments.
However, it is the target of the evocation that is more
indicative of the essential difference of symbolism from
Romanticism, and of Mallarmé's role in symbolist
aesthetics. "Etat d'âme" or "mood" is a composite,
hybrid emotion. Whereas emotion in its simple categories can be represented allegorically (love, fear,
anger, etc.), a mood, consisting of a number of amalga-
mated emotions of the complicated ego, cannot be
identified with a single, circumscribed object. Therefore, when Mallarmé was proposing that the poet
should *suggest* rather than *name* the object, that was
his way of protesting against any word that gives dimensions to objects and puts them within the direct
grasp of every man; in confining the object (a particular bouquet) he robs the perceptive reader of the
possibility of expanding the symbol (the generalized
notion of flower) [6] to suit his mood.

For Mallarmé, then, symbol meant the opposite of
representation, suggestion the opposite of designation:
what is designated is finite, what is suggested is Orphic,
i.e. oracular, for like the oracle it can contain multiple
meanings. "There must always be an enigma in
poetry," as he stated in the same interview with Huret.
Mallarmé liked the word "Orphic"; on the eve of the
official establishment of the Symbolist *cénacle* he was
writing to Verlaine, in his autobiographical letter, that
he wished to give an "Orphic" meaning to life. "The
Orphic explanation of the Earth," to which he aspired
in envisioning the "Great Work" was far out in its

[6] Cf. Mallarmé, "Variations sur un sujet," *ibid.*, p. 368.

grandiose dimensions, quite in contrast to the intimate, sotto voce chamber poetry that was to loom in Symbolist circles. Aside from Laforgue's contemplations of the moon, Symbolism was to be confined strictly to an indoor sort of poetry, and a vision turning inward rather than outward.

It is possible that if Mallarmé had been asked to name the new school he might have called it: *Orphic poetry*. For in these words are implied multiple factors, both of form and of content, and Mallarmé never separated the one from the other. A language that is obscure for the sake of being obscure defeats the task of achieving oracular significance. For Mallarmé the word "obscure" has a purely subjective connotation. When a journalist is obscure, he is defaulting in a domain where it is necessary to have unequivocal reporting; the nature of journalism demands the use of words that leave only one meaning for all and suggest no doubts. When a poet is accused of being "obscure" he is in reality being told that he is not being journalistic; according to Mallarmé, if he did narrate and describe like a journalist, and thereby became clear, by virtue of that very clarity he would no longer be a poet. His so-called obscurity is the public's recognition of the veiled meaning—the only valid distinction between poetry and prose, in Mallarmé's opinion; here is how Mallarmé's English friend Edmund Gosse reports in his "Symbolisme et M. Mallarmé" Mallarmé's very strong sentiment in this respect: "no, dear poet, except by awkwardness, I am not obscure, as soon as people read me in terms of the principles I maintain, or as an example of the manifestations of an art which happens to utilize language, and I become obscure, it is true, if people are misled and think that they are opening the pages of a newspaper." [7]

Orpheus was a musician as well as a poet. This im-

[7] This passage has been translated from Ruth Z. Temple, *The Critic's Alchemy* (New York: Twayne, 1953), p. 213.

plies that the creators of the myth of Orpheus realized the interrelation between the power of music and the power of words in the oracular enigmas that were the nucleus of the poetic form. In restoring the Orphic vision, Mallarmé bade the poet find a form closer to that of music. His definition of "song" is in truth a combination of the visual and the dream: "the contemplation of objects, the image flying out of reveries inspired by them, that is what *song* is." In the light of this concept of music, his inquiry into musical form was much more sophisticated than that of Verlaine. He was not after the *sounds* of music but wanted to recapture the *form* of music. Like Baudelaire, he suggested that music was something more than pleasure accorded to the ear. Music not for pleasure's sake or for emotion's sake, but to set in movement or provoke the imagination—what Baudelaire called "an ecstasy made up of rapture and knowledge," what Mallarmé identifies as that junction of sight and hearing which becomes abstract understanding! There is music and music, as there is musical sounding verse since time immemorial, and poetry grasping that character of music which releases us from the need for logical comprehension and leads us toward the universal Idea.

Let us not forget that the mid-nineteenth century was also the time of the influence of Fabre d'Olivet and his nostalgic longing for the universal language lost for so long to humanity. If the universal language could not be restored, music seemed second best because, in its very resistance to direct discourse, it provided for the transmutation of subjectivity without the intervention of logical meaning. The success of the parallel is inherent in T. S. Eliot's statement many years later that "genuine poetry can communicate before it is understood." Verlaine, though, comprehended the musical parallel only in a very limited way: he thought of this music in terms of syllables and rhymes. But for Mallarmé's more complicated mind it was not the imitations of the sounds of music that were to be most fruitful but the anatomy, the structure of theme and variations, replacing logistic progression. There was more than a joke in the anecdote of the encounter between Mallarmé and Debussy, when the composer said to the poet that he had set "L'Après-midi d'un faune" to music, and Mallarmé replied: "Oh? I thought that I had done that myself." In truth, what separates Mallarmé's poem from the numerous others of the time—it was a very common subject of the period—is not the idea, nor even the words (all of them good Parnassian favorites), but rather the structure, in which narration and description of events are replaced by principal and secondary attitudes serving as channels of varying degrees of identification of the subject's desires with the object of his desire. Image is superimposed on image, transposed from one level to another, as from one key to another; there is a rising and an ebbing, and silences, like musical rests. Identification with longing, like the dynamics of music, measures for each reader in terms of his own private target the distances that separate the reality from the dream and suggests a point—represented by a verbal image for Mallarmé, but which someone else might carve in stone—the point at which art poses its compromise. He made such compromises ever so begrudgingly, and all too often preferred the uncompromising white page. Reading "L'Après-midi d'un faune" like a musical composition, we are far, nonetheless, from the simplistic sound effects of sibilants or resonating nasals; neither counting the syllables nor transliterating the meaning of the words will give the true dimensions of Mallarmé's analogy with music as communication. The musical parallel also helps to explain the symbolist paradox between spontaneity and calculation. For if music is derived from a natural, spontaneous propensity which cannot be simulated any more than can the state of mind of the poet, the calculation of the poem conceived is as tight and accurate as that of musical composition—in both cases an intellectual, mathematical process, rather than an instinctive reaction to an emotion.

In his article on Richard Wagner ("Rêverie d'un poète français," 1885), Mallarmé sensed that Wagner was the ideal of the intellectual musician with whom the image of the true poet could be identified: "an odd challenge he gives to poets, whose duty he usurps with the most candid and splendid bravura." Although the subject of Richard Wagner was one of the most common in his famous Tuesday gatherings, unfortunately Mallarmé had never seen a Wagnerian performance, as had Baudelaire, whose enthusiasm he accepted as a legacy. Actually, when Mallarmé associated poetry with music, he was taking a new look at music, as well as at versification, and implying as much criticism of the former as of literary language. In his Oxford lecture he defined their relationship as "two forms of the Idea." And in 1894 he summarized this position, saying: "Music joins Verse, starting with Wagner, to form Poetry." [8]

Perhaps the most telling of Mallarmé's pronouncements relating music and verse was the statement he made to the artist Degas, which he wrote down later in *Divagations:* "It isn't with ideas but with words that one makes a poem." In other words, as in the case of music, the intellectualizing does not occur in the *content* of the poem, any more than the composer decides to convey this or that ideological message in his composition, but in the *formation* or construction of the poem, which is a calculation just as musical composition is a mathematical code. Valéry's likening of the work of the poet to that of the engineer derives directly from Mallarmé, as the true comprehension of the symbol notation which his disciples had overlooked almost completely. Thereby, according to Mallarmé,

verbalization renders vision as abstract as musical notation which makes heard sounds abstract. The purity
of poetry then, is like the purity of music, in that in
the successful poetic composition the natural objects
disappear into their verbal generalizations, just as in
a musical composition it becomes, except for deliberate
effects, impossible to identify natural sounds.

Therefore, the symbol, according to Mallarmé, is not
the spontaneous and somewhat ambiguous image that
we identify with Verlaine's sceneries and the ensuing
landscapes of the Symbolist poets, but the luminous
products of a conscious battle with the various concrete
facets of reality (whence the use of much concrete vocabulary), their decimation and synthetic reconstruc-
tion into a nondescript, pure totality from which all
kinds of personal emanations can be derived. He said
in *Variations sur un sujet:* "A quoi bon la merveille de
transporter un fait de la nature en sa presque dispari-
tion vibratoire selon le jeu de la parole, cependant;
si ce n'est pour qu'en émane, sans la gêne d'un proche
ou concret rappel, la notion pure."

⊙

George Moore, watching Mallarmé surrounded by
his admirers between the years 1882 and 1894, remarked
in his *Memoirs of My Dead Life* that the *cénacle* could
be likened to the picture of Christ surrounded by his
disciples, and that, to go a step further, the disciples
stood out on the literary horizon like Peter and John,
because of their association with the Master. True as
this may be, the fact remains that when we read today
their manifestoes and ideas about poetry, we discover
that they seem to have misunderstood entirely what
the Master meant. They adopted the notion of the
parallel between music and poetry, in much the same
way as some hi-fi enthusiasts approach the world of
music today. They are so involved in hearing and de-
taching instruments, so concerned about the physical

transmission of the sound, that they lose sight of the harmony and the quality of the patterns. They are so enraptured by the sound of music that they become deaf to the powers of conceptual release and of imagination that are the major riches of musical creation.

The same thing happened to the Symbolist school, which was created at about the time Mallarmé was teaching his concepts of versification and music. The young Symbolists took account of the new importance given to the word in terms of the "high fidelity" of the word's sound, rather than of the imagist capacity of the word as symbol. They became virtually drunk with the power of the word and, by extension, with the power of the verse form. They turned, as René Ghil so proudly stated, into "Instrumentalists," rather than musicians, in the creative sense of the word. As one reads, one after the other, the many treatises written during the years 1886–1890, one is amazed to see how much of the theory is concerned with the outer form of the verse rather than with its intellectual workings.

Mallarmé's disciples went directly into renovations of verse based on their notions of the character of music. They translated the notion of the "tone poem" as "musical verse." That Mallarmé was not particularly concerned with the versification forms that poetry might take is evident in the statement he made which jumped the gun on all degrees of innovation, by taking the most drastically liberalized view of poetic license: he simply stated that any effort toward stylization was poetry. He himself early in his career, in *Igitur,* had gone from alexandrine into cadenced prose. His very last poem, "Un coup de dés jamais n'abolira le hasard," defies in its novelty of form what we call prose as well as what we call verse. Yet, in the interim he did not shun the alexandrine when it suited him.

But his followers ventured immediately into technical innovations: a sampling of their pronouncements will reveal that they sidetracked the issues that Mallarmé had raised. In 1885 Gustave Kahn had assumed direction of the review *La Vogue,* which was to publish the most important of the Symbolist works, including— what was perhaps to become its greatest service to the literary world—the publication of Rimbaud's *Les Illuminations.* As director of one of the official organs of Symbolism, Kahn's voice became one of the most authoritative, although it helped to perpetrate many a misunderstanding about the nature of symbolism. His analysis of verse, stanza, and the construction of the poem as a whole is a far cry from Mallarmé's postulates:

What is a verse? It is a simultaneous stop in the thought process. What is a stanza? It is the development by means of a sentence in verse form, of a completed point in the idea. What is a poem? It is the focusing, by means of the prismatic facets that the stanzas become, of the idea as a whole, which the poet wanted to evoke. Free verse, instead of being, as in old verse, lines of prose cut up into regular rimes, must be held together by the alliterations of vowels and related consonants. The stanza is conceived by the first verse, the most important one in the verbal evolution. The evolution of the thought engendering the idea of the stanza creates the particular poem, or the chapter in verse of a poem in verse.[9]

It is clear that when Kahn put the *idea* at the basis of the poem he missed the issue entirely. He made the poem an intellectual communication, whereas it was evident that, in Mallarmé's thinking, the poem was to emanate from an object or a vision, which words, put together to harmonize like notes in a musical composition, would convey in a generalized, multimeaningful manner. Here we start, on the contrary, with an abstract thought, which is then broken down into subdivisions, which are equivalent to stanzas; in obliterating rhyme, we substitute something just as artificial as rhyme: the studied *sound* relationship of words to

9 Jules Huret, *Enquête sur l'Evolution littéraire* (Paris: Charpentier, 1891), pp. 394–96.

each other, rather than their evocatory, sensory relationship predicated by Mallarmé. The total structure of the poem becomes a bundle of concretions of the original abstract thought, rather than the reverse dreamed of by Mallarmé: the abstraction or purification of the initial, natural form of the vision.

Rémy de Gourmont, a critic of Symbolism, speaking of Kahn's important collection of poems, *Les Palais nomades* (1887), observes as Kahn's most noteworthy contribution to French metrics the Symbolist poet's recognition that French, like other languages, has syllabic accent, a fact which has long been overlooked. He gives credit to Kahn for having returned French to an accentuated verse pattern, for having discovered the distance between meter and rhythm, and for having been a pioneer in exploring new metrical combinations. Today, unfortunately, if any of Kahn's poems are read, it is not for their metrical originality but for an occasional successful image conveying the delicacies of feeling, evoking a stylized medieval climate or the frailty of human beauty. In his *Promenades Littéraires,* Rémy de Gourmont had no intention of damning Kahn with faint praise; but although he commended the theorist's progress, as he thought, in the domain of versification, he did sense that, at the bottom of all the varied efforts of the Symbolists, there was a lack of unified purpose and an impression of chaos: "all the lights vie with one another and continue to produce night."

Another Symbolist theoretician, Jean Moréas, who was Greek by nationality but had become a French poet by election, agreed wholeheartedly with Gustave Kahn, and sought renovations in a return to medieval verse forms and in the use of irregular verse length preconized earlier by Paul Verlaine in "Art poétique": the odd number of syllables rather than the even twelve of the alexandrine. Strangely enough, he hardly practiced what he preached, so that there is nothing particularly baroque in his classically inspired neoparnassian poems.

Two Americans, Viélé-Griffin and Stuart Merrill, prolific in poetic imagery and remarkable in their versatile use of the French language, unfortunately viewed Symbolist poetry as a problem in sound fidelity. Stuart Merrill, in writing *Les Gammes* (scales) in 1887 which, by its very title shows where the poem stood in his view of poetry, aspired to grant French poetry the euphonious character of English verse. In a letter to Viélé-Griffin in 1887, he said: "I am not the only American who is trying to introduce in the French alexandrine a little of the enchanting music of English verse. To express the idea with the aid of words, to suggest emotion by the music of words is the Alpha and Omega of our doctrine." [10] Indeed, if it were so, more the pity! Reading the phrase "To express the idea with the aid of words" makes one feel like the teacher who thinks that he has explained clearly some difficult principle, and then finds the pupil reciting exactly the opposite of what he said. Mallarmé was not talking about the sound of words, nor was he planning to express any ideas in poetry. Merrill is here giving an antidefinition of poetry. And he develops his theory further by suggesting that so far the poet had imitated only small instruments—flutes, harps, and violins—and that the real instrumentalization of poetry was yet to come. Was he thinking perhaps of "big bells and little bells"?

Picking up the well-worn notion of correspondence and synesthesia, Merrill gives it the most superficial application, suggesting the coloring of vowels and images tinted by the sound of the words that evoke, according to him, special sensations. His compatriot Viélé-Griffin praised the *vers-libristes* for having reintroduced the tonic accent into French poetry, and

10 Guy Michaud, *Message poétique du symbolisme* (Paris: Nizet, 1961), p. 774.

went on to prove how varied and flexible French verse could be if the alexandrine, without being abolished, became only one of many meters to be utilized. Strangely, although Viélé-Griffin wrote prolifically in variable metric forms and demonstrated a fantastic knowledge of French vocabulary and structure, his linguistic ability was never matched by poetic sensibility. Euphonistically beautiful, even at times exquisite, the images soon become tedious, as winds whine, shadows shiver, phantoms fawn at the feet of fountains—and Viélé-Griffin emerges as a second-class Verlaine.

In truth, if any Americans were to set examples for the renovation of French verse, it was not to be these two hard-working versifiers, but one already dead, who, without ever having heard of symbolism, was able to convey, even through translation, the breadth and power of verse mutation which echoed the wild rhythms of his savage heart: Walt Whitman, who in terms of his publication in France was a contemporary of the Symbolists. Translated by Jules Laforgue, his *Leaves of Grass* appeared at the same time as the works of the Symbolist *cénacle,* to prove, by deed rather than by word, that irregularities and deviations in verse ring true only when they represent the individualism of the poetic spirit.

◉

It was at about this time that José María de Heredia went to France from Cuba. Upon observing all the foreigners at work on the French language, he remarked: "I am surprised to note that it is the Belgians, Swiss, Greeks, English, and Americans who want to renovate French verse." [11] This was not entirely true; there were Frenchmen who were just as adamant in their false emphasis. René Ghil's *Traité du Verbe* was

[11] Cf. P. Mansell Jones, "Whitman and the Origins of the Vers Libre," *The Background to Modern French Poetry* (Cambridge: Cambridge University Press, 1951), p. 136.

taken more seriously than any other manifesto of the time, even soliciting words of praise from the Master. In paying tribute to René Ghil, Mallarmé summed up Ghil's aspirations by stating that he was trying to construct "a verse as removed from the constant mold as from prose, unreducible to either of them, viable—what an extraordinary honor in the history of a language and of poetry!" So spoke Mallarmé. But when we go to Ghil and read there: "If the sound can be translated into color, the color can be translated into sound and immediately into the timbre of an instrument. The whole discovery [of symbolism] lies there," it is unbelievable that this mechanical little feat could be taken for a major revolution—and by so refined a mind as Mallarmé's.

The further we read into the *Traité du Verbe,* the more amazed we are that Mallarmé could accept Ghil's definition of Symbolism. We must, suggests Ghil, write not only for sense but also for sound. Would not Mallarmé have answered "neither for sense nor for sound"? To say that "language is scientifically music" is to be unaware both of the nature of music and of the nature of language. Language is governed by subjective usage; music is mathematical notation. Ghil's colleague and most estimable, prodigiously prolific poet, Henri de Régnier, also agreed that the important thing in poetry was rhythm and the manipulation of the stanza. In fact, although both Rémy de Gourmont and Gustave Kahn say that Symbolism consists of a variety of manners, all of which agree to reject the old forms, this seems to be the greatest fallacy of all. The fact of the matter is that no one says in reply, that versification is perhaps not the heart of the matter. Instead, they all agree that it is. Even the Master does not protest.

George Moore and Paul Verlaine—neither of whom is in the mainstream of the Symbolist school, but sideline observers—seem to have been the only ones to

protest. George Moore had gone to Paris in the late
1870's, had sat at Mallarmé's hearth, the lamp on the
table, had talked about Symbolism with him and his
disciples. Yet when it came to describing his experiences in *Confessions of a Young Man* in 1888, he spoke
in a mock-serious tone that was quite different from
the sober, self-involved, self-conscious proclamations
of the disciples: "What is a symbol? Saying the opposite of what you mean." Moore talks about Ghil, "who
has added to the difficulties of symbolism those of
poetic instrumentation. And did you know that Rimbaud was mistaken; *A*—green, no yellow!" (As if it
mattered.) And "that man Gustave Kahn who takes the
French language as a violin and lets the bow of his
emotions run at wild will upon it." He has the courage
to call the so-called innovations "verbal eccentricities."
Moore's accounts completely lack the reverence and
awe that pervade the comments of Arthur Symons. Unfortunately, however, literary criticism has long preferred Symons' scale of values to that of George Moore,
and consequently far too many pages of well-docu-
mented literary history have been devoted to writers
who could be summed up in a few short paragraphs.

Among the French, Verlaine protested where Mallarmé seems to have acquiesced. Verlaine deplored the
fact that what was happening was not French: "It is
not verse any more, it is prose, and sometimes it is only
nonsense. And above all, it is not French. We are
French, for God's sake!"

Mallarmé's protest came in a more subtle way. His
"Variations sur un sujet," written in 1895 at the re-
quest of the Symbolist journal *La Revue Blanche,* is a
curious, contradictory document. He starts out as a
Symbolist, with a school tie, and without expressing
any direct protest or criticism ends up by showing that
he means something quite different. The article starts
by showing that Verlaine had prepared the metrical
revolution of Symbolism: "language as a whole, ad-

justed to the metrical form, recovering therein its vital divisions, escapes, according to a free disjunction, into a thousand simple elements; and I will indicate in what follows that it is not unlike the multiplicity of the cries of an orchestration, which remains verbal." In what follows he compliments, in roll-call fashion, the Symbolists: Moréas, Viélé-Griffin, Kahn, Morice, Verhaeren, Dujardin, Mockel. But once he has done his duty, he goes back to his own personal and much more subtle notion of music. He points out the suggestive power of the new music, its ability to skirt the domain of conceptual, non-descriptive thought, and he suggests the parallel work that is possible in poetry, not imitative of the old notions of music, but in line with the progress made in the writing of musical form, suggestive also of relationships in the domain of vision (image), of effects of one image on another, such as the thunder in the forest, rather than the notion of thunder and the notion of forest. If he gives precedence to word over thought, it is not for their scanning potential but for the possibility of mobilizing "the shock of their inequality"; finally, ever so gently, ever so politely, ostensibly without hurting anyone's feelings, he defines the music of verse: "it is not by means of the elemental sonorities of the brasses, the strings, the woodwinds— undeniably not—but from the intellectual word [he uses the word 'parole,' which is the spoken word] at its apogee that Music must result, with plenitude and evidence, as the totality of the relationships that exist in all things." In other words, the poem, like the new music, must break down the barriers that exist between images, barriers that prevent the grasp of relationships. In that undescribed but suggested relationship, according to Mallarmé, lies the poet's sole power to create.

This cryptic bit of criticism, as difficult to decipher as Mallarmé's poetic writings, is however not as dramatic an answer to the Symbolist disciples as the final poem he wrote, "Un Coup de dés jamais n'abolira le hasard," where there is absolutely no music in the sense in which the Symbolists understood music. In fact, the words he chose are strident, much too often disturbingly ungainly in their sound. He went far beyond the free verse of his disciples, obliterated the stanza to which they attached so much importance, played them the neatest trick of the century, by answering their varied sonorities that gave one uniform melody, with a tuneless poem, rich in innuendoes and so cleverly elusive of interpretation that any effort to "understand" it would dispel all the intellectual "ennui" which was symptomatic of the Symbolist climate. Poor Arthur Symons did not have the slightest notion of what Mallarmé was aiming at when he said that Mallarmé would become clear as time passes. To explain or clarify "Un Coup de dés" is tantamount to explaining a tone poem by Richard Strauss or a piece of abstract painting. The sense is variable, the form is as clear and computable as that of a tone poem by Strauss, as one might expect in accordance with Mallarmé's dream of a poetry "premeditated and architectural."

In "Un Coup de dés" the confrontation of man with his destiny is channeled prismatically along four lines: (1) The vague and indifferent "gouffre" that engulfs man is suggested by a whole series of word images, associated with his frailty and his impotence. (2) Man's will to cast the dice despite the overwhelming impersonality of the cosmos is illustrated in the symbolizations of human effort. (3) The futility of the act is intimated by images of spiritual shipwreck, as Mallarmé asks questions which refer to the possibilities of his survival as man and as artist. Negation confronts his venture as the fragments of sentences spell out the non-image: shipless, penless, useless head, empty act, futile game, no release save in empty laughter. (4) The final theme is the destiny of the thought as a faint light of a faraway constellation casts a flicker of hope. Perhaps, in spite of all, the message thrust into space will prevail. From the possible, we have moved to what he calls "this supreme conjunction with probability." The present participles with which he conveys these hopes —watching, doubting, rolling, shining, meditating— contain a tinge of possibility, which injects a somewhat more positive tone into his answers to the questions he asked earlier. Finally, the theme resolves itself into a mild but positive denouement: "Toute Pensée émet un Coup de dés" (All Thought is a Casting of the Dice).

In this verbal calculation, which approximates the transcription of musical harmony, the image or symbol has become vestigial; rather, the words chosen are now self-contained images, used not in logical relationships but as notes that form a chord in music. If in a generalized way Mallarmé represents man's challenge of the void—his message thrust into space, its destination as unpredictable as Alfred de Vigny's bottle in the sea— whatever evocations we may personally have in reading or reciting the poem are purely private dimensions, unshared by others, even as no one can know how things look to other eyes than his own. Mallarmé seemed to have concluded that the most generalized images are the most particular ones, because they can become the most private—and not merely intimate, as was the case with the Symbolists. The well-meaning *explications* that have been proffered since his time tend merely to demonstrate to what degree Mallarmé's intent has been foiled; inversely, the measure of his success as a poet can be gauged by the extent to which we remain dissatisfied with the exegeses.

In this instance, music is far from being the sensually pleasurable and personal song of the Symbolist poets, which, as Mallarmé himself said, is the domain of passion and dreams; instead, he has chosen to simulate the structure of a symphony, a challenge purely to the imagination and the intellect. Already far beyond the instrumentalizations of the Symbolists in this sense, he worked in "Un Coup de dés" for the relation of the visual and the tonal as if he were anticipating an oral execution of the verbal notations on the page: the size of the print corresponding to the time-value of notes; the separations between the words to the pauses in a line of music; and the simultaneous visualization of words on a page suggesting chords, the effects of which would be imitated by choral reading, as of a musical cantata.

A few young poets of the early part of the twentieth century understood that Mallarmé was trying to draw upon the structure of music, an effort far more subtle and significant than the mere borrowing of musical sound. Henri Barzun, as the head of the Orphic movement in poetry in France, was as direct a descendant of Mallarmé as the latter-day Symbolists, and his dream of simultaneity in writing and of the rendition of a cosmic collective poetry was closer to the dream of Mallarmé's Orphic vision than was the intimate, introspective, confidential, monaural poetry of the Symbolists.

As far as the heritage of symbolism was concerned, the theme of "Un Coup de dés" was to be taken up again by Valéry in "Le Cimetière marin," along with the glimmer of optimism which formed a bridge between Mallarmé's last viewing of the frightening "gouffre" and his young disciple's final echo: "Il faut tenter de vivre." But the structure of "Un Coup de dés" fell outside the Symbolist technique. It remained on an experimental basis, as an art of oral poetic rendition rather than as a literary school. The Orphic choir has had some success, particularly in America, under Barzun's long leadership. Ironically, however, despite Mallarmé's tremendous prestige and widespread fame, his dream of Orphically structured poetry, of which he gave a single but masterly example, never became part of the mainstream of symbolist prosody.

When Gustave Kahn suggested in his *Symbolistes et Décadents* that in 1885 there were more "decadents" than Symbolists, he was implying that the true Symbolist was the technician, while the "decadent" was the dilettante who merely breathed the spiritual climate of melancholy and "ennui." He suggested that the term "decadent" had been fabricated by journalists to define a mood; he no doubt considered this popularized characterization to be akin to the one earlier applied to the Romanticists: "le mal du siècle."

If, however, the fortune of Symbolism were to have depended on the importance of the novelties of its versification, it would have had a rapid demise, as indeed it did have in France. What gave symbolism, in its generalized sense, longevity and a power of radiation was that quality called "decadence," and the ability to convey via the symbol-image the mood of mysterious, metaphysical restlessness and the lyrical sense of doom, by a European association of poetic talents, surrounding the French coterie in the final years of the century. The uses of the symbol rather than the uses of the verse form became the crux of the matter; and certain symbols, through common and frequent usage, became a kind of Morse Code, forming a new poetic literacy and establishing a series of literary conventions which we shall note in the next chapter.

THE CONVENTIONS OF SYMBOLISM IN EUROPEAN LITERATURE

Symbolism is a style; it is a signature. The greatest mis-understandings about it have arisen because of the impressionistic criticism by which it has been described. We have noted in previous chapters that among the heterogeneous miscellany of elements associated with symbolism there are three prevailing constants: am-biguity of indirect communication; affiliation with music; and the "decadent" spirit. Guy Michaud, the historian of Symbolism, contends that after 1891 the doctrine of symbolism no longer brings anything new, that it is fixed and congealed. I do not believe that this is true. In the early 1890's, symbolism came to the crossroads; it had some choices to make. It had to choose between the private poetry of Mallarmé and the intimate poetry of Verlaine; between music as it was understood by Mallarmé and as it was elaborated by the *vers-libristes;* between a personal narcissism and the cult of the Universal Ego. If the 1880's were the time of the artisans and technicians of Symbolism, the 1890's were a time for the mingling of the symbolist technique with the "decadent" spirit on a universal and cosmopolitan scale.

If earlier, Swinburne and Moore had come as observers and sympathizers, and the two Americans,
Viélé-Griffin and Stuart Merrill, had become French
Symbolists, as had the Greek, Moréas, and the Belgians,
Verhaeren and Maeterlinck, a second wave of foreign
poets arrived in France after 1890, not to participate
in French Symbolism, but rather to turn symbolism
into an international movement. Between the years
1890 and 1900 we find Charles Morice introducing
Arthur Symons to Verlaine, and Symons introducing
Yeats to Mallarmé. Yeats finds the playwright Synge in
Paris in 1896. Edmund Gosse is also there, in the role
of intermediary. He and Symons will introduce symbolism in England, whereas Yeats and Synge will add
symbolist strings to their harps. From Spain came the
Machado brothers, Manuel and Antonio, and Miguel
Unamuno to spend the closing years of the century in
Paris. D'Annunzio arrived from Italy in 1897, and he
was to stay in Paris for fifteen years; Rubén Darío came
from Latin America in 1892, and much of his poetry was
shaped in the aura and the poetic terms of the Symbolist
school. The German Stefan George, having previously
corresponded with Mallarmé, also spent much time in
Paris while he was editing *Blätter für die Kunst,* his
own periodical, and contributed as well to the Symbolist periodicals of Paris. Through his influence the
Austrian Hugo von Hofmannsthal was introduced to
the Symbolist movement, and we shall see to what
extent he too assumes characteristics of symbolism.

Many others can be mentioned, and many details be
given. These are known facts, and it is not my intention here to review the history of symbolism. But out
of these facts that point to the cosmopolitan character
of the literary relationships that were created around
symbolism there is one interesting factor that needs
to be emphasized. The second influx of foreign writers
into France is different from the first; these later ar-
rivals do not attempt to become French Symbolists, as

did the earlier ones, but rather adapt symbolism to their own national character and literary traditions. For some of them, the symbolist manner and attitude will be a passing phase; for others, symbolism will have a lasting imprint. Out of these writings in French and in imitation or adaptation of the French, there will grow during the last years of the nineteenth century and the early years of the twentieth a series of literary conventions [1] through which symbolism (with a small "s") emerges from the narrow fold of the French Symbolist school and becomes a European movement that eventually will extend to America and as far east as Japan.

First let us see what happens to the dream of creating indirect communication between the poet and the élite audience with whom he chooses to share his vision. As we saw in Mallarmé's work indirect expression became so devious that his poetry turned into something totally private, between himself and God. No one among those who diligently listened to him was prepared to go as far. Most of the poets around him preferred the intimate world of Verlaine, where the meaning may be veiled, the biographical allusions elliptical, but communication is not wholly obscured.

Edmund Gosse, in describing Mallarmé's poetic world in his recollections, *Leaves and Fruit,* said: "All life is still to Mallarmé; his genius, profoundly veiled, haunts a chilly region, glaciers, lilies, swans, and dia-

---

[1] As we illustrate these conventions, I am well aware that, for every example given, many more could be added. As I consider translated poetry "hearsay" poetry, I shall cite only those writings that I can read and understand in their original language. Although I am fully aware that there are some beautiful examples of symbolist poetry in Greek, Russian, Hungarian, Swedish, and Norwegian literatures, I shall have to limit this study to the Western European languages with which I am familiar.

If the examples quoted are of uneven character, it is because, in the search for literary conventions, one is apt to find the most glaring common denominators best exemplified in mediocre works; genius has a way of avoiding literary conventions or of transforming them into something more personal.

monds." Once, in "Symphonie littéraire," Mallarmé
had vividly sketched the topography of his poetic landscape, which he believed to have risen directly from
his reading of Baudelaire: it contains twisted trees
whose bark corresponds to a cluster of exposed nerve
ends, and the intimacy between the image and the
nerve endings was expressed as a "plaintive cry as
of violins which, arriving at the extremity of the
branches, tremble as leaves of music. . . . mournful
basins cut into the flower beds of an eternal garden:
. . . dead, metallic water, heavy brass fountains where
sadly falls a bizarre ray, full of the grace of faded
things." [2] It was almost the only instance in which
Mallarmé's description was direct. The symbolists
thereafter made free use of these regions and of the
swans and of the cold stones, but the code of meaning
they devised through them was more easily interpel-
lated. From them, there emerged a symbolist alphabet.

Only in Italy did the mystery of veiled illusion become an end in itself and produce a wave of hermetic
literature.[3] Elsewhere the verbal ambiguities were minimized; the symbol became a guard, or defense of the
subjective self, rather than a means of mystification. It
even became a short-cut to communication.

There are three types of symbols that can be discerned: natural symbols; mythical symbols; the fusion
of the abstract and the concrete. Natural symbols, such
as the ones that Edmund Gosse mentions, are multiplied astronomically. There are so many swans run-
ning the gamut of the poet's desire to express purity,
virginity, emptiness, sterility, and all the nuances of
the beautiful but cold void! (By the time we reach
Yeats there will be not one, but nine and fifty of them
in *The Wild Swans at Coole.* Finally the Mexican poet
Enrique González Martínez suggests that it is time for
someone to "wring the neck of the swan!") Birds in

2 Mallarmé, *Oeuvres complètes* (Paris: Bibliothèque de la
Pléiade, 1945), p. 263.
3 Cf. Francesco Flora, *La Poésia ermetica* (Bari: Laterza, 1936).

general assume mysterious emanations of the imponderable spirit. Other portentous birds include crows,
seagulls, and nightbirds, as in Maeterlinck's "Serre
Chaude": "Des oiseaux de nuit sur des lys [4] Un glas
vers midi"; in German, there are the dark moths and
wild bees of Stefan George, and in Spanish, hundreds
of butterflies. These are all emissaries between two
worlds; as the little girl says, in Ibsen's play, once the
wild duck has been at the bottom of the sea (the recognizable emblem of "le gouffre"), it can never act the
same again. There are other animals as well: a she-
wolf in Antonio Machado's imagery, dolphins in
Hofmannsthal's.

To Mallarmé's glaciers and barren trees were now
added other rarefied wastelands, halls, stars, caverns,
fountains, mirrors, palaces, hothouses (*Serres Chaudes*
is the title of Maeterlinck's verse collection). Remembering no doubt Verlaine's park—"solitaire et glacé"—
in "Colloque sentimental," which he had translated,
Stefan George describes his own garden, the garden of
the dark, moody emperor Algabal in the section of
Algabal called "Im Unterreich:"

Mein garten bedarf nicht luft und nicht wärme:
Der garten den ich mir selber erbaut
Und seiner vögel leblose schwärme
Haben noch nie einen frühling geschaut.

Von kohle die stämme: von kohle die äste
Und düstere felder am düsteren rain:
Der früchte nimmer gebrochene läste
Glänzen wie lava im pinien-hain.

Ein grauer schein aus verborgener höhle
Verrät nicht wann morgen wann abend naht
Und staubige dünste der mandel—öle
Schweben auf beeten und anger und saat.

---

[4] Maurice Maeterlinck, "Serre Chaude," from the collection
Serres Chaudes (Bruxelles: Lacombiez, 1890).

Wie zeug ich dich aber im heiligtume
—So fragt ich wenn ich es sinnend durchmass
In kühnen gespinsten der sorge vergass—
Dunkle grosse schwarze blume? [5]

All these symbols suggest in various degrees of intensity, the desire to escape, not *to* a new abode but *away from* a place that is distasteful to the poetic spirit. The elements of water suggest desires for purification. Infertile lands are as a release from the futile productivity of earth; they are, at the same time, mirrors of the desolate state of the poet's soul. To what degree the symbol represents the inner condition of the writer, and to what extent it is a means of escape from his subjective antipathy toward the natural world, is hard to determine; in fact, the harder it is to determine, the better the use of the symbol is, and the less it can be confused with simple allegory.

Often the same poet is successful to varying degrees. For example, the colonization of the moon in Laforgue is the symbol of all that is arid and unreachable: but two excerpts from "Litanies des derniers quartiers de la lune" readily show the difference between the oblique implications of the symbol and the almost allegorical explanation of it.

Hôtel garni
De l'infini . . .

Léthé, Lotos
Exaudi nos! [6]

You can read into those short lines a thirst for the infinite or a desire for forgetfulness and for sensuous dreams; the ratio is not indicated, but ripples of con-

[5] Stefan George, *Algabal,* Gesamt-Ausgabe der Werke, Vol. II (Berlin: G. Bondi, 1928), p. 96.
[6] The quotations from Laforgue used in this chapter are from Jules Laforgue, *Oeuvres complètes* (Paris: Mercure de France, 1922).

jecture are set in motion in the mind of the reader. In the same way, one can figure out the degree of release and discovery implied in the last line. On the other hand, consider the following lines from the same series of poems:

Astre atteint de cécité, fatal phare
Des vols migrateurs des plaintifs Icares! . . .

Astre lavé par d'inouïs déluges
Qu'un de tes chastes rayons fébrifuges

Ce soir, pour inonder mes draps, dévie,
Que je m'y lave les mains de la vie!

Here the discourse is very direct; the meaning is unilateral, personal, and subjective, leaving no room for doubt or stipulation on the part of the reader. In an unequivocal allegory, the moon corresponds to the non-life; its blindness parallels the poet's desire to lose his human senses, so that he may rid himself of human existence. The qualification of this poem as symbolist verse is possible only in terms of its irregular versification and its "decadent" spirit, certainly not in terms of the use of symbols.

◉

Gradually these much used symbols, even though they were ambiguous at first, were becoming fixed and specific by the extent to which they were being shared by a long series of authors. If at first they had a multiplicity of meaning, stylization was reducing their ambivalence and the character of their enigma. Their monotony lent itself to the type of satire that is inherent in Laforgue's *Moralités légendaires:*

Il était un roi de Thulé
Qui, jusques à la mort fidèle
N'aima qu'un cygne aux blanches ailes
Voilier des lacs immaculés

Most of the symbolists were conscious of this pitfall. Maeterlinck expressed astutely the distinction between the effective symbol and the artificial one. Without limiting his observation to his own period, he said that he could discern two kinds of symbol: the *a priori* symbol, which starts with an abstraction and tries to give it a human vestment, thus coming close to allegory, and the other type of symbol, which has a much more unconscious character, comes almost without the awareness of the poet and, instead of representing his thought, transcends it, survives it, furnishes thought for all time to come; the degree of genius in a writer determines the extent to which he can produce the latter type of symbol.

The symbolists soon realized that they were being marooned in metaphoric conventions, and tried to find escape from them. As the inner landscapes lost their equivocal character, so did the use of color and the color-tone synesthesia. Symphonies in grey, white, blue quickly took on clear-cut correspondences doubling for emotions: red for anger, blue for imagination, grey for melancholy, etc. Pan's flute in Mallarmé and Verlaine's violin that sobbed, were not only used over and over again, but a series of other instruments were added, to communicate the range of delicate emotional innuendoes on the part of the symbolist poet: clarions, harps, guitars (particularly among the Spaniards), bells, death knells, and finally, many years later, the harmonium of the American, Wallace Stevens. The use of these instruments produced a chromatic scale of subjective moods that were easily recognizable; as in the case of the visual landscapes, the auditory symbols became readily identifiable and lost their quality of mystery.

What recourse was left? In European literary history each time a writer exhausts his inventiveness, he takes refuge in the myths of the past. The end of the nineteenth century had been a time of revived Hellenism, with the discovery of the Venus of Milo and much excavation in Thrace. Under the instigation of such Hellenophiles as Moréas, the Hellenic landscape was brought back, as a second source of symbols, but in a manner quite different from that of the Parnassians. In the poetry of Leconte de Lisle there had been an attempt to reconstruct the Greek age, to emulate its ideals, to revive its cult of beauty. In the poetry of the Symbolists, the Greek symbols were put to a much more personal use. As Jacques Rivière was to aptly observe, many years later: "The Greece of today's poets has nothing left of the classical. It is a land of dream where they go to play with the nymphs."

Pan, the nymphs, Sappho, Diana, Leda, the Lotus-eaters, Ariadne—all had been much in vogue; by mid-century they had become very tired symbols. The Symbolists made of them the ambiguous population of their dreams, emphasizing their unreality in the every-day world, rather than their ever renewable messages. Each time one of these characters appeared it was a signal that the poet had left the world in which he breathed and transported himself into the imaginary, timeless landscape of mythology, there to mingle his mortal senses with the unearthly senses of these figures. To those already known were added a series of less utilized names, such as Proserpine, whose connection with Death and Life at the same time represented the fatal alliance of the poet himself. A tremendous re-newal of subject matter resulted from the re-utilization in ambiguous form of the Greek myths. To these were added other mythological figures; some, inspired by Wagner, such as Lohengrin, Elsa, Parsifal; other medi-eval characters, such as Mélusine; Yeats added the Celtic ones, more mysterious because less recognizable by the general public.

The purpose of the myth was twofold: on the one hand to create an aura of mystery; on the other, to find an equivocal medium of reference. Unfortunately, the

pitfalls here were as many as in the case of the lilies
and the grottoes of the inner landscape; for Moréas and
Régnier in France, for Hofmannsthal, George, and
Hauptmann in Germany, the classical allusion ceased
to function as an intermediary symbol and loomed as
an end in itself, thereby reducing the so-called symbolism to a neo-classicism. The spiritual identity of the
fairy figures in dramas such as the *Sunken Bell* became much too clear and created a duality between
the physical world and the imaginary one that tended
to be artificial and precise. Celtic symbols fared somewhat better but unfortunately were to be too often
explained away by the rational annotations of eager
literary historians.

The most successful form of the symbol was that
created by the fusion of the concrete or physical reality
with the abstract or inner mood. The following example from Maeterlinck's *Serres Chaudes* is easily
recognizable today by readers anywhere, whatever their
particular frame of reference, for it is a poetic device
that prevails far into the twentieth century:

Mon âme a joint ses mains étranges
A l'horizon de mes regards.
Exaucés mes rêves épars
Entre les lèvres de vos anges!

Very often, as in Moréas' "Le Pèlerin passionné," nature becomes one of the arms of the metaphor in this
type of imagery, sealing its correspondence with the
inner self of the poet in the manner made famous by
Verlaine's weeping violins:

Triste, les pâles lys de la mer natale;
N'est-ce ton corps délié, la tige allongée
     Des lys de la mer natale!

O amour, tu n'eusses souffert qu'un désir joyeux
Nous gouvernât; ah, n'est-ce tes yeux,
     Le tremblement de la mer natale!

The same technique prevails in works far removed from the scene of the Symbolist coterie. The Dutch poet J. H. Leopold (1865–1925), who wrote a poem of homage on the occasion of Verlaine's death, provided many examples of this symbolist mingling of the material and the spiritual, as in the following poem:

O, wat in loten
van welig blij zijn
in denken u bij zijn
was uitgeschoten,

trok in tot klauven
die smartend grepen,
van wild benepen
bloedend berouven [7]

O, what chanced to be
Wonderfully happy
In thinking you near
Has slipped away

Pulled into the claws
That smarting clutch
Of wild, timid,
Bleeding regret

Flowers also have this double connotation of concrete and abstract in parallel series in the poem "Antifona" by the Brazilian poet José da Cruz e Sousa (1861–1898), called the Black Swan of symbolism. The poem, first printed in the collection *Broquéis* in 1893, ends with:

Flores negras do tedio o flores vagas
De amores vaos, tantálicos, doentios . . .

[7] J. H. Leopold, "Verlaine," in Theodoor Weevers, ed. *Poetry of the Netherlands in Its European Context*, 1170–1930 (London: The Athlone Press, 1960). This volume was brought to my attention by Fred J. Nichols, a graduate student in Comparative Literature at New York University, then professor of Comparative Literature at City University of New York, Graduate Center.

Fundas vermelhidões de velhaz chagas
En sangue, abertas, excorrendo en rios . . .

Tudo! vivo o nervoso o quento o forte,
Nos turbilhoes quiméricos do Sonho,
Passe, cantando, ante o perfil medonho
E o tropel cabalístico de Morto . . .

In short, regardless of the particular means used,
those poems can be said to be distinct from the Romantic if they have been able to make effective use of
equivocal discourse in a number of ways: the unusual
word, the object, the landscape, the myth, the coupling
of abstract and concrete characteristics whose relationship is not ascertained—all these devices being attempts
to transcend direct meaning and to open up the vistas
of conjecture, to raise the limited experience of man
the poet and man the reader to a level of multiple
possibilities. This objective was one of the main common denominators of European symbolism. If the results appear today like a series of partial defaults, the
reason in large measure is that the conventions became
so widespread, so universally embraced and utilized,
that they were not able to allow much margin for
originality.

How did the affiliation with music, which had been
suggested by Baudelaire and Mallarmé, fare on the
European scale at the end of the century? The flexibility of rhythms that would convey musicality to
words was the model followed by poets who had
learned to employ symbolist expression in various languages. In the Spanish lilt, the German regularity of
versification, the English translations by Symons, the
emphasis is on the music of the word itself rather than
on the function of the poetic line.

German regularity of versification was preserved on
the whole, as Stefan George put the emphasis on the
power and music of the *word* rather than on variations of prosody. In Arno Holz' "Mittelachsenpoesie"

we see how linguistic experimentation can produce word-building and sound-accumulation at the same time, in the construction of the image as a form of synthetic communication. Such a word picture is "Barocke Marine," and its rather unusual conjuration of a sea nymph:

> Auf
> blanken
> Delphinrichenfinnen
> muschelempor,
> hoch
> ein Weib!

The permissiveness of the German language with regard to the creation of new words as needed gives the German poet a wonderful freedom that is barred to poetry in other languages.

Even without knowing the language one can sense the play on the sound and music of words manifest in such a sampling of Russian symbolist-inspired verse as follows:

> Moi mily mag, moya Mariya
> Myechtam mertsayushchi mayak
> Myatezhny mareva morskiye,
> Moi mily mag, moya Mariya.
> VALERY YAKOVLEVICH BRYUSOV

> I sama ta dusha, shto pylaya, zhdala
> tsvela nochnaya tishina
> A. A. BLOK

> Lila, lila, lila kachala
> Dva tel'no-aleye stakla.
> Belei lilei, aleye lala
> Bela byla ty i ala . . .
> FEDOR SOLOGUB

Variation rather than change seems to be the tendency. As for writing verse in order to evoke a state of non-verbalized imagination, Mallarmé's feat was never duplicated; there was to be only one "L'Après-midi d'un faune" and only one "Coup de dés." But Mallarmé's aesthetics seem to have given to Claude Debussy new insight into the nature of music. In setting "L'Après-midi" to music, Debussy had indeed liberated music further from recognizable affective patterns and opened a path for purely imaginative, non-descriptive mood settings, with a highlighting of new instruments, that suggested a mystery untouched by religious allegory. He was to do the same thing on a broader scale for Maeterlinck's *Pelléas et Mélisande* and to initiate a new style. There were others inspired by the symbolist poets: Fauré, Duparc, Ravel, and the powerful Richard Strauss.

As we shall notice later on, the symbolist aesthetics was to influence the drama form much more than the purely poetic form, despite the varieties in verse pattern that were tried out. It seems apparent, as we observe the evolution of poetry from our vantage point, that even without the work of the symbolists, the prose poem and free verse would have developed anyway, building upon the examples set by Baudelaire, Poe, Whitman. In fact, the exaggerated melodiousness of the symbolists provoked a reaction in Laforgue, and later in T. S. Eliot, which swung the pendulum all the way over to prose, not for its musical freedom but for its colloquial simplicity, in protest against the ornate meanderings in sound of free verse.

Paul Valéry, commenting on the historic significance of symbolism in the development of poetry, has said that "there is no symbolist aesthetics," and also explained that "their aesthetics divided them, their ethics united them." [8] He justly stresses the fact that the promises of the renovation of the *form* of poetry were not really fulfilled. What he calls ethics, however,

8 Paul Valéry, "Existence du symbolisme," *Oeuvres*, Vol. I (Paris: Bibliothèque de la Pléiade, 1959), pp. 690, 694.

is the symbolist view of life and of the world, which we have been trying to crystallize as the "decadent" spirit. On the European scale, the aspect of symbolism that proved most lasting and viable was the composite of attitudes and moods suggested by all these forms and all these symbols. If at a certain point in the development of the movement, critics were justified in separating "symbolist" from "decadent," everything points to the fact that in the last ten years of the century the two become so intertwined that without the "decadent" spirit there would be little left to distinguish symbolism from Romanticism. As we look from afar at the tremendous output of poetry and sift this vast body of writings through the measures of time, it becomes apparent that those poems are truly beautiful, prevailing, and haunting, in which the deliberated expression is indeed a means for conveying the quality of that despair that is inherent in "decadence."

Once again the poets were faced with a choice—between being neurasthenic, engaged in an excessively morbid cult of the personal Ego, lost in dreams and hallucinations like the hero of Huysmans' *A Rebours*, and giving a greater stature to their meditations on mortality by turning the personal preoccupation into a contemplation of the Universal Ego. Here the case was clearly in favor of Mallarmé. His greatest field of influence was to be in the suggestions he left, through his personal demeanor and in his writings, for the delineation of the "decadent" spirit: the withdrawn manner, the concern with the mystery of life, the futility of free will, the imminence of death in man's daily existence, the abyss of our incomprehensions—but, with it all, the consciousness of the role of the artist, the comfort of the arts as the only means of demolishing chance, the permanence of man through the emission of a thought. In accepting this position, the symbolists demonstrated a deeper philosophic mettle than Verlaine, or Oscar Wilde's Dorian Gray. The mirror, which had been the symbol of the contemplation of self, became the representation of the void, the absence of life, or gave way to the white sheet upon which the poem might blossom. If "decadence" was basically the haunting awareness of man's mortality—"the daily tragic," as Hofmannsthal calls it; "the tragic sentiment of life," as Unamuno expressed it—then the impermanence of the artist as creator was overcome by the permanence of the created work, and nihilism was able to negate itself through the work of art. What Rimbaud had earlier discerned, in the distinction he made between the egotist and the creative artist, became the true gauge of the validity of the symbolist work of art. Does the so-called probing of the soul consist of the dazzling effects of synesthesia, or of the great flight into solitude, or of the togetherness of the elite, or of consolation in alcohol and/or drugs? Or do the images of death and devastation, of the cruelty of time and the frailty of man, transcend the narcissist preoccupation and achieve a representation of the human condition? The best of the symbolists achieved this end.

Maeterlinck and Laforgue set the tone for the new metaphysics, which consisted of a heightened awareness of the void in which man navigates blindly, not knowing where he comes from nor where he is heading. Laforgue's symbol was a "bark of nihilism." Verhaeren characterizes men searching for their destiny as fishermen "isolated in the depth of mists"; and Rubén Darío's "false azure," expressed in "Tarde del Trópico," represents his anguish and bitterness ("angustia" and "amarga" are two of his favorite words), his preoccupation with the abyss and the weeping of the waves:

Del abismo se levanta la queja amarga y sonora
La onda, cuando el viento canta, llora.

and the feeling of being always a passerby: "sentirse pasajero." In a poem called "Nocturno," he conveys this malaise of the bitter defloration of life, its vast grief and the trivialities of small worries. In "Lo fatal" he expresses the futility of man's fate: "there is no greater sorrow than to be alive. . . . that is to be and not to know anything. . . . not to know where we are going and from where we came!" It is a statement that so many of the poets of the epoch have made and put in the mouths of their characters.

All the myths that could signify this hopelessness of man's destiny were utilized. In this respect, the myth of Hamlet, so attractive to this end-of-a-century attitude, is hardly identified with the Shakespearean character struggling within himself, but has been stylized into the moment of contemplation of Yorick's skull. This is the Hamlet who identifies man as the "quintessence of dust." From one end of Europe to the other, under the banner of symbolism, poetry became a *danse macabre,* in which death, the great and formidable intruder, waits in the shadows, mingles with us, takes his mask off at the least expected moment. One sees this in the work of Hofmannsthal. In "Der Tor und der Tod" Hofmannsthal says:

Der Tod ist überall: mit unsern Blicken
Und unsern Worten decken wir ihn zu

(Although we hide death with our eyes and with our word, it is everywhere.) In "Der Weisse F'ächer" he explains:

ich weiss, dass der Tod immer da ist
Immer geht er um uns herum
wenn man ihn auch nicht sieht
irgendwo steht er im Schatten und artet
und erdrückt einen kleinen Vogel
oder bricht ein welkes Blatt vom Baum.

Death is always there, hidden in the shadows, communicating its presence through a little bird or a fall-

ing leaf! Life slips between one's fingers, says Hofmannsthal; it is nothing but a shadow-play ("Die
Leben ist nichts als ein Schattenspiel").

There are many personifications of death, going beyond the imprecision of symbols to the clarity of allegory: Rubén Darío's queen of nothingness, for example, with a bouquet of roses made of stars, or
Jiménez' infinite butterfly. But death is not always
personified in beauty; often it takes on horrible pos-
tures and grimaces, hides behind masks; in the most
artful representations, such as Maeterlinck's *L'Intruse,*
its passage rather than its presence is suggested, by its
effects on mortals rather than its confrontation.

A direct result of the hypersensitive awareness of
death is a tendency to withdraw from the life force as
a humble manifestation of free will. From this angle
it is interesting to note what happens to the love theme
in the curious treatment that symbolists give to love.
Already in Baudelaire's last love poems a distinct
change could be noted. Abandoning both the notion of
spiritualized, idealized love, and that of voluptuous
love, when he came to the "Femmes damnées" Baudelaire equated love with the elusiveness of the dream.
A close reading of the poem reveals that the inversion
on the part of the "damned women" is really a fear of
love rather than the erotic fulfillment generally attributed to the followers of Sappho. Their withdrawal
from normal love seems to have been prompted by fear
of the brutality of life:

Va, si tu veux, chercher un fiancé stupide;
Cours offrir un coeur vierge à ses cruels baisers;

We are not far from Mallarmé's *Hérodiade,* where
Salome is not the seeker of vain pleasures but a human
shadow, annulling the life-surge as she looks at the
world through a mirror and cannot bring herself to
face it squarely:

J'aime l'horreur d'être vierge et je veux
Vivre parmi l'effroi que me font mes cheveux
Pour, le soir, retirée en ma couche, reptile
Inviolé sentir en la chair inutile
Le froid scintillement de ta pâle clarté
Toi qui te meurs, toi qui brûles de chasteté,
Nuit blanche de glaçons et de neige cruelle!

The same withdrawal from life in the spirit of the "decadent" is discernible in Laforgue's *Moralités légendaires,* where Hamlet rejects Ophelia as the life force in favor of the purity of nothingness, where Salome, Diana, Lohengrin, Pan, and the Syrinx, all become expressions of a nihilistic rejection of life considered as a waste of energy. Salome is pictured as "le parfum des gaspillages et des hétacombes nécessaires" (the perfume of all that is wasted and of the inevitable hetacombs), in other words, the symbol of waste and death. For Laforgue, who represents the epitome of the "decadent" spirit, even the enticement of the dream is not a real escape. He answers Mallarmé's "L'Après-midi d'un faune" with: "Et la légendaire poursuite de la nymphe Syrinx par le dieu Pan continue dans l'accablante après-midi qui finira par se fondre en soir." (The afternoon has indeed become night, assumed the cold infertility of the end of day, which in its ramifications is also end of love, end of aspiration, end of world.) The tubercular Laforgue is afloat on his bark of nihilism. If "happiness is the pursuit of an ideal, and nothing more," as the Syrinx says, then the relinquishment of the ideal is the end of the road. And so early and so often Laforgue arrives at this impasse! He berates the goddess Diana for conserving useless sex organs, and makes Lohengrin chide Elsa for any tendency she may have to be libidinous. And when Lohengrin finally takes flight on the feathers of a pillow changed into a swan, it is to reach the metaphysical altitudes of love where the breath of no maiden can tarnish the pure mirrors of the glaciers. Note that where in general, the young girl is taken as the symbol of purity, even in Mallarmé's *Hérodiade,* Laforgue goes further and shuns the symbol of purity as a source of impurity in potential form, precisely because it contains the life-creating force:

> . . . l'oreiller changé en cygne éploya ses ailes impérieuses et, chevauché du jeune Lohengrin, s'enleva, et vers la liberté meditative, cingla en spirales sidérales, cingla sur les lacunes désolées de la mer, ou par delà la mer! vers les altitudes de la Métaphysique de l'Amour, aux glaciers miroirs que nulle haleine de jeune fille ne saurait ternir de buée.

He sings the apotheosis of the Lily as symbol of "the Mecca of polar sterilities."

It is to be noted that this "decadent" spirit of the latter-day symbolists is not a moral deviation, but a mystique that has lost its religious props. The religious meaning of "soul" has been replaced by an awareness of the universal psyche of man, lost in the physical world that he will never comprehend. The Brazilian Cruz e Sousa expresses this state of being as "saudade," which suggests a combination of longing, nostalgia, and detachment from life; untranslatable, "saudade" contains the meaning of such associated words as "retiro," "erme," "deserto," "sentâo," and "solidâd" all at once. It becomes the poet's mission to represent man as shrouded in this earthly mystery, to picture him as a victim of forces over which he has no control. The remedy is not escape to another point in life, but withdrawal from the very rhythms of life altogether. D'Annunzio summarized this attitude in very apt terms in 1912 in his *Martyrdom of Saint Sebastian:* "One must struggle to develop to its highest point the sense of isolation and impermanence. One must little by little break all the ties which bind one to life, and which involve such a waste of precious energy. I know of no more distasteful epithet for a man than to call him happy." [9]

A very delicate balance holds together the "decadent" spirit and the symbolist image. Often the images of rarefactions are represented either by the spiritualization of the living or by the embodiment of the ethereal, mysterious powers that surround mortal man. When they are not backed by the "decadent's" anguish to a sufficiently high degree, the symbols become stylized, and eventually monotonous. The danger that faced the French Symbolists was the tendency to become marooned in their own metaphoric conventions. On the other hand, when the "decadent" could not succeed in channeling the curse of being a mortal into an art image, but expressed it in terms of the personal ego, the result was not the poetic alchemy of symbolism, but philosophy set to verse. This seems to have been the pitfall of many of the German poets. Stylized imagery on the one hand, tendency to versified abstractions on the other—these were the flaws of symbolism that were to become part of its legacy to twentieth-century literature. But despite these pitfalls, which produced unevenness among the writings of this large group of European poets, they recognized in the spirit of symbolism a mutual affinity such as had perhaps never appeared in any of the earlier literary movements.

What drew foreign poets to the Paris school was the recognition that the Paris of the artist was as remote from France as it was from England, Germany, or any other bourgeois nation of the contemporary world. The writers found solidarity in their isolation from the rest of humanity, in their withdrawal from the life current; they sought poetry as the last stronghold of

[9] Mallarmé had said virtually the same thing in a letter to his friend Henri Lazalis in 1863: "To say 'I am happy' is to say 'I am a coward' and more often 'I am stupid'."

the disinterested cult of beauty. There was drama in
their poetry, the drama of their own personalities ne-
gating the harsh world about them.

The fact that so many diverse national elements
mingled in the development of the symbolist movement does not make of it a cosmopolitan movement:
by the word "cosmopolitan" it is suggested that it belongs to the whole world. What symbolism really did
was to close its shutters on the world. In reaction
against increased literacy in the civilized world, there
emerged a new literacy of poetic conventions, closed
to those who could find only literal meaning in language. It is true that in creating an international but
esoteric communication among their own coterie,[10] the
poets cut themselves off from the ever-increasing groups
of potential readers that would be attracted to literature. The isolated position of the poet in society today,
his inability or unwillingness to communicate with the
large reading public, stems from Verlaine's decision "et
tout le reste est littérature." The poets of the end of
the century agreed with that verdict to separate poetry
from the rest of literature, and thereby they rejected
the vast audience interested in "literature." They determined the poet's destiny for many years to come.

[10] In the article "Existence du symbolisme," written in 1936
to commemorate the fiftieth anniversary of Symbolism, Valéry's
last words are an observation concerning the persisting isolation
of the poet, an attitude that he associates with the basic symbolist ethics: "Never did the ivory tower seem higher."

VII

THE SYMBOLIST
THEATER

*"the play written in the
folio of heaven"*
—MALLARMÉ

In histories of the symbolist movement not enough
attention has been paid to the theater that stemmed
from it. Although there have been a number of interesting studies of the symbolist theater of Lugné-Poe,
they have considered the subject from the point of
view of theatrical development rather than of poetry,
and from within specific national confines rather than
from a non-nationalistic vantage point. In this connection, Haskell Block's study *Mallarmé and the Symbolist Drama* [1] measures Mallarmé's talents in terms of
dramatic criteria, and although Professor Block clearly
perceives Mallarmé's shortcomings as a dramatist, he
opens the way to studies whose purpose may be other
than to judge symbolist theater in terms of what it
fails to do as traditional theater; the principal interest
should rather be to ascertain to what extent it succeeds
in twisting the arm of dramatic convention in order to
direct theater to fresher fields, in which the mid-
twentieth-century dramatic artist is better adapted to
thrive.

Here, however, in examining the symbolist theater

[1] Haskell M. Block, *Mallarmé and the Symbolist Drama* (Detroit: Wayne University Press, 1963).

of the 1890's neither from the point of view of traditional theatrical form nor as precursor to avant-garde
theater, but as poetry, as one of the forms—perhaps the
most successful, in view of the homogeneity of its qualities—that the symbolist movement took in Europe, one
notices more familiar traits between the French Villiers
de l'Isle-Adam and the Belgian Maeterlinck, between
the Austrian Hofmannsthal, the German Hauptmann,
or the Irish Yeats than between contemporary compatriots such as Villiers and Henri Becque, whose common national heritage did not include a common
spiritual bond. One of the true and lasting successes of
the symbolist movement was to be the dramatic frame
it created for poetry, which reached out further than
esoteric, intimate verse. Its influence has not ceased
today, for like ripples after the stone has been tossed
it continues to disturb the artist on a broader orbit
every day, reaching beyond the theater to the cinematographic medium.

What better locus for synesthesia than the stage? The
form, the color, the gesture, the accompanying music,
even perfumes (which were injected into the air of
Lugné-Poe's theater, as the incense of this new temple
of man's latest form of mysticism), announced the man-
made correspondences that would replace the marriage
between Heaven and earth. Here was an opportunity
for the graphic projection of the inner landscape onto
the external reality of the world of objects, and of animate beings, none of whom would have any autono-
mous character but would represent the various shad-
ings and fluctuations of the author's mood. What was
this mood indeed but the artist's confrontation of the
void, "le néant," "nothingness," and of its accompanying themes of fear, solitude, the passage of time, the
awaiting of death? Since there is no definite answer to
the great questions and mystery of life, the ambiguity
of symbol and discourse could effectively replace the
conversational chatter of ordinary theater; the defaults

of the symbol, which were represented in the writing of poetry by the white and empty sheet of paper, would appear in terms of theater so much more effectively in vocal silences and verbal interruptions; in terms of dramatic art, they would be so much more telling than eloquent monologues.

The mutations symbolism achieved in verse writing are in effect as nothing to the assaults that it made on dramatic form. But the irony is that it was not the boos of rabble audiences, nor the jeering of journalists, but the logical, studied commentaries of specialists of the drama that tended to berate and in the end to demolish the symbolist theater, *taken on the basis of conventional ideas of what constitutes successful theater.* Was it not one of the precious attributes of theater to present strong, self-revealing characterizations, giving the actor a role to delineate, elaborate, use as a foil for his own rich personality? What is the use of possessing a fine instrument when the music is played in a single modulated octave, when the characters act so alike, when they speak so little, when they wait endlessly for something to happen instead of thrusting themselves against destiny, when they are neither good nor bad, but just sad, and inactive as in sleep? Rilke observed that amateurs could enact Maeterlinck's plays better than professional actors. This remark could apply to any symbolist play, because indeed there is a certain effacement of the actor demanded by the poet-dramatist, who is all his characters and is looking for a medium rather than an interpreter, someone to communicate his words simply, in unified rhythm with the rest of his means of communication which consists of gesture, décor, light, and climate. Here then was "strike one" against the symbolist theater: no characterization and no opportunity for interpretation.

The second defect or default from the point of view of conventional theater was the lack of crisis or conflict in the symbolist drama. Why should there be a

desire to overcome obstacles in life, when the greatest obstacle is death, and it is unconquerable? If there
is an impression of an absence of crisis in these plays,
it is because the crisis is in truth ever-present, and that
continuous presence must be conveyed by a high pitch
of sensitivity rather than by action or by the dynamics
of emotion. The creation of an atmosphere of intense
inner vibrations is as intangible as the power of human
personality itself; but it is as electrifying, when it
exists, and as effectively communicative.

The third defect from the point of view of the end
of the nineteenth century was that this type of theater
contained no ideological message, at a time when the
theater had indeed become a form of pulpit from
which moral issues were preached. No conclusive idea
could be taken away from the symbolist representation. There was no catharsis, because no moral issue
had been thrashed out; neither a play of emotions nor
an exchange of ideas was furnished by these plays.
They neither entertained nor instructed. They fulfilled
none of the aims traditionally connected with the
theater. For that reason they became very easy targets
both for the critic and for the actor. Appraised as
"theater," they fail at every point; to this day they
remain, except in "art theaters," the property of that
same small reading public that enjoys poetry. For indeed their true significance is evident only as a branch
or part of poetry, which in turn has become in our
time a branch of metaphysics and philosophy.

From the point of view of poetry, the symbolist
theater succeeds more often where verse fails to fulfill
its symbolist objectives. The ambiguity of discourse
can be represented by an equivocal relationship between the characters and the objects that surround
them. In the symbolist theater, no object is decorative;
it is there to externalize a vision, to underline an effect,
to play a role in the undercurrent of unforeseeable
occurrences. The interplay of lights and sounds empha-

sizes the correspondences between the physical and the spiritual, so that the time of day, the striking of a clock, the suggestion of wind, the variations of color flooding the stage are a language different to each spectator, just as music will move each hearer in a different manner, according to his temperament and his experiences. The power of evocation on stage came closer to Mallarmé's desire to evoke through words alone the spiritual climates of music. With the aid of gesture and the variations of dialogue, repetitions and silences were much more able to provoke the imagination and help the spectator to reach the dream state than mere words printed on paper, no matter in how diversified a metrical form.

Knowing that a poet, rather than a dramatist, would create the symbolist theater, all eyes were turned to Mallarmé, who as early as the 1860's had announced the genesis of his *Hérodiade* as a tragedy in three acts; he was to devote to this project long, solitary evenings of many years, but was never to bring it to fruition. Even one of the prominent actresses of the time, Mlle. Morino, was prepared to play the role of the virginal Salomé; but the play simply did not come through, and the poem of it that we have is like the stage directions and a scenario. Haskell Block, who sees dramatic power in "Hérodiade," remarks that "Our view of Mallarmé as a poet should not blind us to his real, if limited, dramatic talent." [2] He analyzes "Hérodiade" as well as "L'Après-midi d'un faune" from the point of view of their dramatic characteristics of conflict, action, and visual attraction and shows how, unfortunately, they still missed becoming dramatic compositions.

However, a theater of symbolism did develop, not from Mallarmé directly, but from his symbolist entourage, embodying his dream of the verbal and visual projection and externalization of the ingredients that constitute the power of music: non-rational communication, stirring the imagination, and conducive to subjective vision.

It would be a great temptation to venture into an historical account of the development of the theater of Lugné-Poe in the late years of the century. But the great director of the French art theater belongs to the history of the stage rather than to that of poetry.[3] What is pertinent to the European symbolist movement is the fact that Lugné-Poe had the vision to stage foreign plays that had an affinity with symbolism when true symbolist plays did not spring up instantly or spontaneously from the national literature. Strindberg, Ibsen, Tolstoy, and Shakespeare were in sharp contrast with the local theatrical scene of the naturalistic theater. Lugné-Poe recognized the need for a new concept of theater, and he prepared the ground for symbolist theater by accustoming his audiences to theater as a sanctuary, as a place of meditation rather than predication.

If Mallarmé defaulted, his friend Villiers came through with a play which was at least partially symbolist. *Axël* had been conceived more than twenty years before it was staged in 1894, and there is much in it that is philosophical, Shakespearean, even Romantic rather than symbolist.

In examining *Axël* from the point of view of the symbolist movement let us not forget that it predates Symbolism in the same way in which much of Mallarmé's writings are forerunners rather than consequences of Symbolist aesthetics. From the point of view of structure, *Axël* resembles more the Romantic theater of Goethe, Musset and Hugo than the symbolist theater of the epoch in which it will first be produced. It has

---

[3] Cf. Gertrude R. Jasper, *Adventures in the Theater: Lugné-Poe and the Theatre de l'Oeuvre to 1899* (New Brunswick: Rutgers University Press, 1947).

exposition, crisis, and denouement. It has characters that explain themselves in direct conversation and in clear monologues, much as Hamlet does. The objects around Axël, the prince of the Black Forest, have no ambiguous meaning which might promote a subjective mood in the spectator. If there is symbolism in the dark forest where he drags his melancholy, in the caves of his ancestors where the drama of his life comes to a head, these decors are very simply allegorical and have representative rather than suggestive power. The objects play no roles in the flow of the drama; they are local color, as in the plays of Victor Hugo. There is no latent animism in them; they decorate the places in which the characters wander as they convey in explicit terms their state of mind. As Villiers unfolds the drama of the dark prince, weary of life, who meets a strange maiden seeking refuge in the sepulchers of his ancestors, it is neither in ambiguity of discourse, nor in dramatic structure that Villiers' play is symbolist. It is symbolist, however, in terms of the "decadent" spirit, which it manifests magnificently, so much so that Axël becomes identified as the image of the symbolist hero.

The play is derived from a Swedish source. There was an *Axel* written by Isaias Tégner, the author of the Frithiof's Saga in 1825; the play had been translated into French in 1867, and it is shortly after that date that Villiers is known to have made his first draft of his play. In comparing the interpretation of the characters in the two plays, it is easy to see how different is the Romantic spirit from that spirit of "decadence" which Villiers' character crystallizes. Both Axëls are orphans, trained by tutors for the arts of war; and both prefer meditation to action as if in a spirit of perversion. Both have sensitive natures that prefer the forest to the court life, the silence of their thoughts to conversations with other beings. They each unexpectedly meet an exotic maiden who wants to draw the hero out of his austere surroundings. The

Swedish Maria nurses Axel back to health, and it is an accidental death that comes to mar their happiness, as it often does in the Romantic theater. In Villiers' *Axël,* on the contrary, when Sara invites Axël to venture off into the unknown, he answers that the type of adventure she is seeking is a delusion of humanity. He chooses the anti-voyage, just as Baudelaire did in his final poem "Le Voyage" ("Plonger au fond du gouffre" [4]), and he invites Sara to join him in the only escape that he believes will not prove a deception: death. "Oh, the external world! Let us not be dupes of the old slave, chained to our feet, in the light. Let us go far away from it, briskly, in a sacred leap." The sacred leap is death. The consummation of even the most perfect love will be a pollution of it, Axël believes, in true symbolist spirit, like Laforgue's Lohengrin and Mallarmé's Hérodiade. "Live? our servants will do that for us," he tells his beloved as the wedding bells ring for Ukko and Luisa, who are in his service. Axël and Sara commit suicide, as the only voluntary act of which a human being is capable, after they have had their moment of spiritual love for each other, untainted by any physical act. "The real accomplishment, absolute and perfect, is the inner moment which we have experienced of each other."

The play had the so-called defects of the symbolist theater, even if it did not have all of its structural earmarks: it was static, somber in mood, sepulchral in tone, suggesting that haunting preoccupation with death that was the principal subject of much symbolist writing. It set the poet off from the rest of humanity; although Axël proves to be an unusual figure —from the point of view of the psychologist, probably something of a manic-depressive—Villiers' art transforms the individual case into a universal figure by turning many of Axël's pronouncements into a syn-

[4] Baudelaire, *Les Fleurs du Mal, Oeuvres complètes* (Paris: Pléiade, 1954).

thesis of the symbolist poet's fear and rejection of the world. Instead of bringing Axël into open conflict with the forces that have made him what he is, instead of making him at last "take arms" against his "sea of troubles," as Shakespeare did with Hamlet, thereby making of that figure a unique individual, Villiers concentrates in this actionless play on the results, the unalterable results, which are applicable not only to this particular Axël, but which could constitute the denouement of so many other endgames. Thus the cult of the "I" transcends mere preoccupation with the personal ego, and instead, it can be identified with a whole area of the human condition, particularly as it was prevalent at the end of the nineteenth century, and which re-echoes among so many artists in the mid-twentieth century.

If Villiers represents the spirit of symbolism, Maeterlinck combines with that spirit the technique of the new theater, which is anti-theater in the same sense as the poem in free verse or prose is anti-versification. A Belgian by nationality, born in Ghent and arriving in Paris in 1886, Maeterlinck said overtly that he owed everything he had done to Villiers. The remark is somewhat excessive, however, unless we consider that without Villiers he might not have ventured into the dramatic form of the symbolist movement. Two short plays of his, *L'Intruse* and *Les Aveugles,* appeared in 1890, and his most famous and universally acclaimed full-length play, *Pelléas et Mélisande,* appeared in 1892, two years before *Axël.* It is significant to note here that the short symbolist play has proved to be more successful in terms of staging and presentation than the longer one, presumably because, depending as the symbolist play does on the sustaining of mood and tension, it is easier to achieve this on a short-term basis than for a longer stretch. In the English theater, the plays of Yeats, Lady Gregory, and some of the short plays of Lord Dunsany and Synge (such as *Riders to the Sea,* 1904), attest to this phenomenon: the secular critics are less apt to accuse these plays of "dragging."

L'Intruse is a jewel of the symbolist theater, absolutely foolproof, and flawless as judged by symbolist standards. Its subject is an abstract one: death itself. The whole setting is symbolist in *effect,* without any specific allocations or materializations of the idea. The symbolization is that of absence, and the passage of the absent force through the décor and among the persons in the décor, all of whom react to its passage, not as separate entities but as a symphonic unit, modulated to each other, resounding in their speech and movement to a single harmony, rather than to any particular or personal conflict. The story is very simple: a group of people, related to one another, are awaiting the death, off-stage, of a woman who is fatally ill after childbirth. She might have been dying of any other ailment; but it is supposed that as childbirth unites the concept of death with that of life, which are considered the only important issues of the human condition, it conjures up the human condition rather more succinctly and totally than other ills. If in analyzing this play we were to think of it as structured on the pattern of a symphony, rather than as a dramatic piece in one act, we could say that the first movement is the waiting, the second is the passage of death through the chamber in which the characters are waiting, and the climax is the impact of death in the room off-stage where the victim lies. There is no struggle; if there is confrontation, it is between the human group and the absent force that passes among them, and makes its presence not seen but sensed.

Now, in a Romantic play, the advent of death might be represented by a character disguised as a human; the specific personification would make of the notion of death an allegorical representation, and perhaps there might then be a struggle if not explicitly represented, at least implicitly suggested as Death made its way among the humans. But in this little play the footsteps of death, the hands of death, the voice of death are suggested, even as Mallarmé had advocated, by the *effect* they produce rather than by the objects that might be made to represent them: the barking of the dog, presumably at the moment when death enters by the gate; a gust of wind; the crying of the birds; the flicker of the lamp on the table around which the group is gathered, when death is actually in their midst; the light from the sickroom when death passes into the next chamber—and these signs are recognized by the members of the group in varying degrees according to their sensitivity.

The most sensitive among them is the blind man: Maeterlinck often attaches greater powers of perception to those who cannot see, thereby implying that in these persons the inner eye may be more highly developed. It is in fact the blind man who triggers the recognition of every significant sign, without ever *identifying* the signs with any definite notion. And we find each sign reaching, like a wave, into the consciousness of each person on stage in varying degrees of understanding, from flat denial of the existence of this undecipherable outside force to partial surrender to it. Not only the blind but also the aged are deemed more perceptive; perhaps as they approach the frontiers of life, they begin to be exposed to emanations from what lies beyond those frontiers. At least, that is what one senses in the gallery of wise old men that Maeterlinck scatters in his plays. Strangely enough, although there are persons of a religious order in the play, they are not pictured as being among the most mystically sensitive members of the group that is witnessing the passing of a soul.

Instead of conflict, there is, as a replacement for movement, a sense of tension, of attitude, the suspense of waiting, the silences that convey the ticking away of time, and the electrifying ending, sudden as it was in-

evitable. An infinite amount of art has to go into the
staging of such a play, a well-timed interplay of sound
effects and lighting shades to hold the mood; else, the
whole play can seem silly and insipid; and the actors,
who have so little to say, may appear lifeless, unless
they too retain the sense of their collective purpose, not
only among themselves but with the inanimate things
around them, which play just as important a role as
they do. So unimportant is their individuality, in terms
of the general theme, that their names could be inter-
changed as could their sex; blindness and various degrees of age are the only determining characteristics.

Maeterlinck's major contribution in the field of symbolist theater was, of course, his full-length play,
Pelléas et Mélisande. Here again, the subject, plot,
and characters are stereotyped and unoriginal. The
play is concerned with the eternal triangle: in this
case, two brothers love the same woman, to whom one
of them is married. There was a verse play by Ludwig
Tieck, called *Genoveva de Brabant,* with essentially
the same cast of characters, even to the name Golo,
which is reminiscent of Maeterlinck's Golaud. We
might say that Tieck's play was pre-symbolist in that
it was concerned with mood, in a nocturnal atmosphere; it had set symbols, such as the Golden Cup; it
played with the idea of the prophetic dream and its
implications for the lives of the characters. But if this
is an example of poetic drama, not all poetic drama is
symbolist theater, even when we see that there is symbolism in lyrical verse, the symbolist character is not
taken in the specific terms in which we have situated
it, historically and stylistically, within the framework
of the Symbolist school and its radiations.

Pelléas et Mélisande begins with a chance meeting
of the hero and heroine and ends with the natural, if
untimely, death of the heroine. The characters have
had no control over either event, nor does the tragedy
result from failure in their human struggles, nor from

the vengeance of the gods. The temporal forces that work out coincidences uncontrolled by man and the physical forces to which man is materially a prey produce the trauma to which these characters are subjected; and it is through their suffering that they come to a sharper awareness of the haphazard nature of human existence here on earth. Their names are arbitrary; they could just as easily be called "Everyman"—but a belated Everyman, ever so much more vulnerable because he has been sensitized by civilization. Mélisande appears on the scene, not knowing where she comes from, nor does she know where she is, nor where she is destined to go, and repeats everything she says three times. As we have already noticed in poetry, this ignorance of origin and lack of destination is one of the symbolist themes pertaining to the destiny of man; it recurs in many of the German plays of the symbolist era, as well as in Claudel's early plays, which are more symbolist than really Christian.

Mélisande meets a prince, the ruler of a mythical kingdom, a widower, who falls in love with her and marries the young girl who has no identity. She has no understanding of happiness or unhappiness, and soon thereafter becomes submissively pregnant, as if unaware of the implications. Soon after, when by chance she meets in the forest another stranger, the brother of her husband, the love that blooms in her is equally unconscious, an attraction that is viewed by the author neither as good nor evil, because there is no moralistic judgment involved in the elemental movements of the "I" traced in the unfolding of the play. A fountain and a grotto are the trysting places; there is the loss of a crown and of a ring; there is a tempest, a fall from a horse; and particularly there is all over a smell of death, even before Golaud kills his brother Pelléas, and Mélisande dies in childbirth.

What are the meanings of these sceneries and objects, these manifestations of the elements of nature?

They have the meanings we may wish to give them;
they are metaphors just as Mallarmé judged the movements of dancers to be metaphorical. If these keys to
the general mood were too clearly highlighted in the
production of the play, it is very likely that the result
would be an old-fashioned allegory and ruin the effects
which hold up on very ephemeral ground. One must
also note that here, as in *L'Intruse*, there is an old man
(the grandfather of the two men) and, in addition, a
young boy, the son of Golaud by a previous marriage;
both of them have more perception and more fore-
boding of things that are to happen than do the other
characters, presumably because youth, like age, is closer
to the unknown that surrounds the rational limits of
human life. Once again, death in childbirth may suggest the continuity of life and death, or their proximity; certainly there is no thought of moral retribu-
tion, as there would be in the allegory of the morality
plays. There is no sense of responsibility nor is there
awareness of sin, for whatever is done happens even as
a storm or a beautiful day. Perhaps what such a play
best defines is man's identification of beauty with his
natural melancholy, and his awareness of the harmony
between his inner perceptions and the manifestations
of the natural world—a harmony that is capable of
reflecting his keenness and the intensity of his vision.

Maeterlinck employed several technical aspects of
the symbolist theater here: the repetition of words,
like the repetition of musical phrases; the echoes from
one character to another, like the answering of one
instrument to the other; the pauses, the enigmatic
character of certain lines, as if possessing the hyp-
notism of a witch's pronouncement. Mallarmé, commenting on the production of *Pelléas et Mélisande*,
spoke of "This art form, in which everything becomes
music in the proper sense." "In the proper sense"
surely implies that it is not its singsong verbal music
but its structural form that he was referring to; he

saw in Maeterlinck's work what he himself had failed to achieve in "Hérodiade."

Other viewers did not manifest Mallarmé's empathy with Maeterlinck's symbolist theater. Judging from the point of view of theater, rather than that of music or poetry, they criticized it in terms of what it was *not* rather than what it was. The reviewer of the *Universal Monitor,* speaking of the characters, said: "Hallucinated, they look straight ahead, far, very far, vaguely, very vaguely. Their voices are hollow, their diction choppy. They strain to look as if they were lunatics. They do this in order to create for us the sensation of the beyond. They would make us dream of the infinite even while we say: 'Nicole, bring me my slippers.' "

Today Maeterlinck's theater is almost extinct, as far as performance is concerned; it survives only in the opera by Debussy, for which it serves as libretto, although the opera is staged seldom enough and enjoys a *succès d'estime* thanks only to the music which suggests to modern audiences the mystery of Maeterlinck's story much better than do the words. Even this is destroyed when operatic actors, unversed in the tradition of symbolism, try to give the words and actions the very aura of reality that the author tried to avoid. Strangely enough, if the modern reader or viewer wished to appreciate the theater of Maeterlinck, he would be better equipped to face certain elements in the so-called avant-garde drama of today, which stem directly from symbolist style; such seems to be the case with Samuel Beckett's *Waiting for Godot,* with the Italian theater of Ugo Betti, and with such cinematographic realizations as Bergman's, Fellini's, and Alain Resnais', of which there will be some mention in the conclusion of this study.

In his own time, Maeterlinck was an avant-garde writer for much of central European drama, exerting an influence on the plays of Hauptmann and Hofmannsthal particularly. Hauptmann had started his literary career as a naturalist and is still best known for his naturalistic plays, such as *The Weavers* and *Rose Bernd*. While symbolism is generally referred to in literary manuals as a reaction or antidote to naturalism, the plays of Hauptmann demonstrate that, in a sense, symbolism is another facet of naturalism, rather than its opposite. The symbolist, particularly when he projects his notion of destiny, is not so far removed from the naturalist as he is generally deemed. Putting aside considerations of style and technique, the two have a certain affinity in terms of their philosophy of life and provide a concerted reaction against Romanticism. It is well to ascertain some of these similarities before considering the theater of Hauptmann, where the two movements seem most clearly to coexist.

Naturalism and symbolism are both nurtured by fatalistic philosophies in which the human will is subordinated to outer influences and pressures. In naturalism, the social and hereditary realities overpower human action and determine human character. In symbolism—as in the philosophy of Schopenhauer, with which it has a strong affinity—it is again forces outside man's power of control that cast him about between life and death, the two poles of mysterious origin, unexplainable to him and controlled by chance. The third external element that fashions the pattern of his life is better known, but is equally beyond his control: time and the objective ticking of the hour, which is so incompatible with man's subjective sense of time, the notion of "duration" which the philosopher Bergson has described in conceptual terms, whereas the poet suggests it by his metaphors. In either case, the deterministic but improvidential character of outside forces takes away from man the notion of purpose, aim, will, the significance of any *coup de dés* he may want to attempt. Both the symbolist and the naturalist are in that sense materialists.

There is neither predetermined providence, nor faith in the hereafter; nor are there correspondences between Heaven and earth, but only between the physical world and the psychic world, which in a sense is determined by man's purely mortal and therefore organic nature. While the naturalist concerns himself with the social behavior of man under the pressure of uncontrollable forces, the symbolist is concerned with man's mental reactions to and reconciliations with the natural order of the cosmos; in both cases, a natural pessimism is inherent, which suggests that, whether as a group (in naturalism) or as an individual (the symbolist hero), man is unable to rise above human existence or even to shape it. This consequently implies the unimportance of individual character weaknesses or strengths, which are the bread and wine of dramatic writing. As compensation for this subordination of conscious moral struggle, atmosphere emerges as an important factor, social and exterior in the naturalist play, subjective and interior in symbolism—that is, translated into either natural elements or fantastic emblems, animate or inanimate. As drastically different as these representations surrounding the human characters may appear, they play the same role—that of externalizing or prolonging the human condition. Maeterlinck mentions in his *Trésor des humbles* "the impossibility of superior life within the confines of the humble and inevitable reality of daily life." This is an apt definition of both the naturalist and the symbolist theater.

A look at Hauptmann's theater will illustrate better than any generalizations these two facets of nineteenth-century pessimism over the human condition. *The Sunken Bell* (1897), which is based on a fairy tale by Grimm, poses as its basic theme a question that we have already met in symbolist writing: the bell-maker, Heinrich, asks: "Where do I come from, whither do I go?" He finds no satisfactory answer in religion and cries: "a curse upon their church and creed!" He is a mystic whom the established religions have failed to satisfy, as was the case with so many artists of that era. However, after rejecting religion he finds his thirst for the unknown so persistent that he is compelled to seek other forms of the marvelous, such as witchcraft. He encounters a mysterious being, reminiscent of Mélisande, somewhat more aware of her mystical propensities, in fact presented to us as knowingly possessing supernatural powers—a twilight-zone character who entices the hero to conceive a bell beyond normal proportions and lift it to the loftiest mountain heights, only to have it fall to the bottom of a lake. Presumably because man is not really worthy of such heights of spirit, his work is doomed to oblivion, just as this bell sinks to the bottom of the lake. The other symbols are not all as obvious and overt as this one. Night, morning, the elements, water-sprites that bring into perplexing view man's concept of the real and the unreal, are actors in this strange drama which is staged in a semi-fantastic world, neither rational nor totally irrational. Even the breach of fidelity, caused by the attention which Heinrich gives to the fairylike child-woman Rautendelein for whom he abandons his wife, is not taken as a moral break but as a metaphysical crisis.

In many of his subsequent plays, Hauptmann studies the role of destiny, the presence of death, the inevitable chain of causality which makes life seem so futile, and man's ominous awareness of a nothingness which puts obstacles in the way of free will and liberty. If many of the characters in such plays act as if irrational, it is because they are concerned with problems that supersede the rational. The ominous phrase in *Schluck und Jan* is "soon you must die." In *Die Schwarze Maske,* death enters the scene in the company of a band of players, wearing a mask, and participates in a banquet. In *Winter-Ballade* we sense the transmission of fear of death, or of something announcing it, when a dog barks (but there is no one there) and when the minister gets up and leaves the table suddenly, without having touched his food; the seagulls bring in something from the sea—we are not quite sure what it is—just at the moment when a female character dies. The setting for *Gabriel Schilling* is a cemetery near the sea (foreshadowing "Le Cimetière marin" of Valéry?) and we see the hero making a coffin, as he is surrounded by seagulls, swans, crows, those emblem birds of the symbolist convention, now playing roles on the stage. There is also in Hauptmann's plays a whole series of child-women, intuitive, unconsciously wise, and reminiscent of Maeterlinck's old men and young children: Hannele, Pippa, etc. Although Hauptmann's philosophical statements are more explicit than Maeterlinck's, he uses many of the same mood-creating devices, such as repetition, broken statement, unfinished dialogue, silence, expressive gesture in place of the word. Much of this drama has been deemed Romantic and Faustian, but let us remember that what sets the symbolist drama apart is the intuitive surrender of character to place and phenomena, and the absence of struggle. This in a sense removes these plays from the category of tragedy, even though they deal with that very "sentimiento trágico de la vida," as Unamuno, a Spanish participant in the symbolist experience, expressed it.

An Austrian also attracted to symbolism was Hofmannsthal, who at eighteen became acquainted with the poetry of Baudelaire and Verlaine. Born in 1874, he might more naturally be considered with his chronological contemporaries such as Valéry, Rilke, Jiménez, except that his symbolist works date from his early writings, whereas in his later works he sought, as did Hauptmann, a classical vein and translated his spiritual conflicts in terms of more specific classical symbols, such as Elektra, Oedipus, etc. In the last years of the nineteenth century Hofmannsthal was much like Rimbaud: a boy poet, mature beyond his years, reading avidly, and establishing literary connections not with his contemporaries but with the older generation. In his letters between 1890 and 1901 he mentions Maeterlinck, Swinburne, Verlaine; he has read *Pelléas et Mélisande* in German in 1897 and has been enchanted with it, as with the earlier *La Princesse Maleine*. In 1900 he meets D'Annunzio in Italy and then moves on to Paris. Hofmannsthal is the eternal vagabond, a man without roots, identifiable with the spiritual ubiquity of symbolist characters, such as we have noticed, without origin or known destination.

He sends his first book, *Der Garten der Erkenntnis*, to Maeterlinck. In interpreting the "daily tragic" he senses that each moment of our life is a crisis; everything is linked in us, just as we ourselves are linked with the outer world, more than we dream of. In *Gespräch über Gedichte* Hofmannsthal grasps two of the most significant aspects of symbolist aesthetics. He notes that words should be made to reveal the power of magic they contain in themselves, rather than used as explanations of any subjective feeling of mystery of the person who utters them: "That is why symbol is the very element of poetry, and that is why it never puts one thing in place of another. It utters words for the sake of words; that is its magic: for the sake of the magic power that words have to stir us bodily and to transform us incessantly." Going one step further, he concludes that "The word is mightier than he who speaks it." It is in fact this observation that he implements in his verse dramas, where many of the utterances of his characters loom larger than the poor humans who speak them. If every moment is a crisis, and the word is more significant than the one who utters it, it is a theater in which creation of character is subservient to the expression of universal truths about what unifies men rather than what distinguishes them, even as "plot" in its ordinary sense negates the idea that each moment is portentous without being extraordinary. The lack of plot leads to a unity of existence before the great leveler, which is Death. Hofmannsthal has been called "Der Dichter des Todes" (the poet of death), and indeed it is his chief preoccupation. He does not fear death as such, but he provides setting after setting for its predominating presence in the activities of men. The *Stimmung* that he creates is in effect the "mood," made up of the same grottoes, halls, corridors, stairs, caverns, castles, birds with souls, and fountains, as we have encountered in symbolist poetry and in the theater of Maeterlinck. He uses the same monosyllabic dialogue, the hallucinated monologue, the masks, the twilights; and in *Woman at the Window* we find in Dianora of the long hair, a counterpart of Mélisande, engaged in actions similar to those of *Pelléas et Mélisande.* Here, as in other symbolist plays, no human adversary can be as formidable as that natural adversary, death. In *Death and the Fool,* which in translation cannot match the magic of alliteration inherent in the title *Der Tor und der Tod* (1893), death takes on the sensual pleasure provided by a musician as he appears with a violin; in his almost completely static, plotless dialogue, Hofmannsthal suggests, as did Mallarmé in *Igitur,* that death may indeed be deemed an experience to be sought and explored rather than feared.

Hofmannsthal was saved from theatrical oblivion in much the same fashion as Maeterlinck: as Debussy transformed the Belgian's play into an opera libretto, so Richard Strauss transformed into stageable opera what might otherwise have been merely reading matter for literary historians. The assistance which each of these authors needed from the musical artist suggests that words as music did not really rise to the level dreamed of in the highest ideals which the symbolists set for their art. Not alone, but with the aid of musical

synchronization, were they better able to achieve that
form of non-conceptual verbal expression which interprets the pathos and beauty of the human dream, thus
avoiding the logical language which in its endeavor to
communicate poetic truth, often destroys it in the
process.

In considering the symbolist theater created between
1890 and 1900, the fact is often overlooked that Paul
Claudel belongs to the group. So closely is his work
connected with Catholicism that one often forgets that,
like T. S. Eliot, he participated in a non-religious
mysticism before his total ç̧onversion to the Church.
In this respect, his two early dramatic dialogues, *Tête
d'Or* and *La Ville,* demonstrate a sharp breach with the
later and much better known works that place him
clearly at the head of the Catholic coterie of the early
twentieth-century French literature.

In 1890, however, Claudel was a young admirer of
Mallarmé at the salon of the Rue de Rome, where he
came into contact with all the practicing Symbolists.
He was not an unconditional convert to Symbolism, as
he has revealed in his correspondence with Jacques
Rivière, for he was at the same time feeling the forces
of Rimbaud and the attraction of Victor Hugo's later,
cosmic poems. In the long run these non-symbolist
forces were to dominate his writings, but the first
dramatic works are distinctly symbolist in technique as
well as in tone, revealing in compelling intensity the
decadent spirit. In 1893 he wrote to Mallarmé: "Let
me congratulate myself for having had the good fortune to encounter at the beginning of my literary
career your conversation, your example, and your
friendship." It is interesting to note that three such
diverse leaders of French thought in the early twentieth
century as Claudel, Gide, and Valéry had all been subject to the same influence in the Rue de Rome and had
called the same man "master" in their youth. Later, to

be sure, they were to take divergent directions in the development of their respective literary destinies.

When, some thirty years later, upon reading the posthumously published *Igitur,* Claudel chided Mallarmé for having been a "decadent," he seems to have forgotten his own *Tête d'Or,* with its series of characters just as diffident toward life as Mallarmé's, as removed from the mainstream, as self-engrossed in their meditations, as inquisitive about the cross-purposes of life and death. The many voices that suggest answers to the fundamental question "Who am I and what is life?" present no conflicts of attitude. They are instead parts in a cantata in which they supplement each other, as they unfold an incoherent story of boredom, illness, old age, and death: Cébès, who has remained fixed to the native ground and has nursed his "ennui" like a long contemplation, without beginning or end; Simon, who has wandered to the four corners of the earth and comes back to observe that all roads, all cultures, all cities pass away, as we pass and are gone. Together they bury a woman who has just died, with the desperate finality, even brutality, of those who have no stakes in the hereafter. Later, Cébès, himself moribund, will meet his brother, Tête d'Or, who comes home as a conquering hero. But he who has conquered other men is equally powerless before death and before his brother's questions. There is only nothingness beyond the grave; man has only his hour and dies. "Don't hope any more!" We die alone, and when we are dead there is no difference between a mole and a man, once the processes of putrefaction set in. "And after having lived, we surrender to the same nameless void, our soul blotted with love and maledictions." A desperate melancholy, nausea, a black flag, a stormy passage, the weight of chains—these are the marks of man's passage. His refuge lies in nursing his gross ignorance in "an august dream" where he has learned "to be married to himself." This is how

Claudel, the young symbolist, viewed life: he envisaged the cult of the self as a wedding ring binding man to himself; it is a chain and yet a protection from the terrifying vulnerability to which he subjects himself when he diverts his vision to things outside of himself and is brought up sharp against the inevitable anonymity of non-self-consciousness. There is also a mysterious princess here, as in the plays of Maeterlinck, who once more represents the self that cannot find its identification: "I do not know who I am" is to be taken not only in its physical, but also in its spiritual sense. Again, as in all symbolist writing, time is the cruelest of enemies. As the first Captain expresses it: "The future is only a landscape mirrored in the water, and the past is worth less than a beach; and the present is nothing at all." Instead of the pathetic fallacy, by which man applies to nature his inner thoughts or sentiments, here it is the sea, the trees, the wind, the dismal objectivity of the soil that create the fatal despair of man.

In his next play, *La Ville,* Claudel tried to give a few answers to the questions that persisted in tormenting him. He sought to arm himself with some weapons against the impending oblivion of death, which again is the recurrent theme. The narcissistic contemplation of the mortal plight becomes more universal as the characters find identification with the group condition (represented by the city), the group activity (represented by the enslavement to daily work), the interdependence which assuages the devastating reality of the total uselessness of the total effort. The drama here is the struggle of man against the void, whereas in the previous play there seemed to be submission without struggle. A character, Besme—so comparable to Beckett's Estragon that it seems unlikely that the resemblance is purely coincidental—repeats in hypnotic fashion: "Nothing is." When pressed to explain what he means, he defines "nothing" as the depth of all things, which totally eludes the capacity of our minds. But Claudel makes concessions to the poet's lyricism, admitting that it can partially overcome—at least temporarily—the bleak mystery in which man is engulfed: "You will explain nothing, o poet, but through you everything will become explicable." At the end of the play, he goes so far as to lift his voice gently against the "decadent" spirit:

> . . . man is not made to turn his face toward the sea as if toward a mirror
> From the limitless abyss of the waters rises, in the night a vertigo, and in daytime the terror and the dream
> But the earth beneath his feet asks to be tilled
> And the sky above him yields to a precise astronomy.

In other words, to the inaction of man in the ivory tower, Claudel responds with the efforts of man's hand and the calculations of his mind as challenges to the futility of all action and all thought. Yet in technique he is still very much the symbolist, condemning this play, as the previous one, to the repertory of unperformable theater. No action accompanies the spoken word, which takes the form of long monologues, or a most unconversational dialogue, interspersed with silences. These speeches are projected onto a vast, cosmic canvas where indeed nature is an open temple and its pillars—such as the tree, the vine, the wheat—are deemed to have meanings only partially revealed by the poet; even as the parts of the day form a meaningful parallel to the variations of human mood; to the end of his long career, Claudel was to attach a certain sense of spiritual crisis to high noon. There are also symbolic objects, such as the table, the ring, and mystical gestures, as of sharing or kissing. Lights and costumes could undoubtedly be used as special effects to highlight the critical moments of a drama that is in appearance so totally static.

Perhaps because so much of Claudel's future dramatic writings will be laden with emotional conflicts and intense confrontations of divergent human wills, these two early plays bring out the more strikingly all that distinguished symbolist theater. How shattering it was to conventional dramatic composition! How vulnerable it made itself, when it gave up the role of entertainment or of emotional catharsis, and instead put all its characters, as it were, into the same boat— or rather, shipwrecked vessel!

⊙

Although Yeats, at the turn of the century, attempted in English the same impossible feat of writing symbolist drama, he openly and somewhat apologetically admitted the impracticality of attempting to stage his plays. Whereas Mallarmé had tried to place "Hérodiade" and "L'Après-midi d'un faune" within the technical orbit of drama and to overcome thereby the barriers between theater and poetry, Yeats conceived his own dramatic verse, not as theater, but as an extension of poetry.

Yet, in whichever of our thematic-chronological divisions we include Yeats, he will disturb pedantic organization. Though he is loath to define his dramatic form as theater, this aspect of his work falls much more within the framework of the symbolist spirit and technique than his pure verse. It seems impossible to overlook it in any consideration of symbolist theater, although the composition of most of Yeats' plays postdates by a few years the cluster of works that announced the symbolist theater. Despite their chronology, they cannot be allocated to the "afterglow" into which his early twentieth-century contemporaries fall. His plays are indeed part of the zenith of symbolism.

As we have previously noted, Yeats was witness to the development of French Symbolism and among the international enthusiasts who surrounded the *cénacle*.

He was in the audience at Lugné-Poe's production of *Axël,* sharing with that audience the belief that theater could be a new temple of mystical contemplation. Supporting Mallarmé's attitude that the poet in the modern world had no alternative but to seek refuge in the substitute religion of art, he made his thought explicit in two articles on symbolism, "The Symbolism of Poetry" and "Symbolism in Painting." [5] In 1897 we find this young friend of Arthur Symons asserting, in "The Celtic Element in Literature," the vitality and universality of the symbolist movement: "The symbolical movement, which has come to perfection in Germany in Wagner, in England in the Pre-Raphaelites, in France in Villiers de l'Isle-Adam and Mallarmé, and in Belgium in Maeterlinck, and has stirred the imagination of Ibsen and D'Annunzio, is certainly the only movement that is saying new things."

We may also note that in this same statement, although Yeats was fully aware of the coterie meaning of Symbolism, he gave the movement a much broader frame of reference: historically, he extended it to include Dante, Blake, and Burns, and nationally, he encompassed most European literatures; in terms of artistic categories, he included within the same symbolist aesthetics the musical imagination of Wagner and the dramatic imagination of Ibsen and D'Annunzio, not as cause and effect, or as origin and influence, but as simultaneous phenomena, nurturing a basic mystical need in Western civilization.[6]

Mallarmé had dreamed of a new Sacred Book; in

[5] The quotations from Yeats' essays used in this chapter are from W. B. Yeats, *Essays and Introduction* (New York: Macmillan, 1961).

[6] In another essay, "The Autumn of the Body," Yeats gives his own definition of the "decadent," containing the symbolist spirit by extending it to a more universal plane: "I see, indeed, in the arts of every country those faint lights and faint colours and faint outlines and faint energies which many call 'the decadence' and which I, because I believe that the arts lie dreaming of things to come, prefer to call the autumn of the body."

"The Celtic Element" Yeats vaguely attributes the notion to Mallarmé's Belgian disciple, Verhaeren, and is inspired to seek in legend the mainspring of the symbol: "The arts by brooding upon their own intensity have become religious, and are seeking, as I think Verhaeren has said, to create a sacred book. They must, as religious thought has always done, utter themselves through legends. . . ." The Celtic legend, closest to him, becomes the core of his dramatic writing.

We have observed that the forces of life and death cause magic encounters, which are represented through a prismatic vision of the non-situated, non-identifiable presences in Maeterlinck's plays, or by stylized recreations of Greek myths, or of fairy figures of undetermined ethnic origin in other symbolist theater, or simply as exotic names to cover the non-corporeal fusion of memory and dream, as in the figures of Axël or Rautendelein. In Yeats' dramatic works, these forces and their effects are incorporated into Celtic legend, which becomes the base of his own Sacred Book; in it, the Druid, in his invisible everlivingness casts the magic of dreams and enchantments on men and women to make them aware of the paucity of their measured time and the shallowness of their material props.

As with Maeterlinck, on Yeats' barren stage it is the old and the blind who have the greatest insight, who most readily seize the link in the universal duality and correspondence between matter and spirit, between the visible and the occult, between sound and silence, between presence and absence. Like Hofmannsthal, Yeats adds the fool to the list of perceivers; like Claudel, he brings the vagrant into the charmed circle of the feeble and the useless who, in his opinion, possess more power than the strong and the important. In *Cathleen Ni Houlihan,* the old woman who interrupts the prenuptial celebrations is of unknown origin and destination, as is typical of symbolist characters whose non-identifiability is indeed their best means of identification. The old woman crosses the path of the young man who is about to be married and lures him into her absent world. When she vanishes with him and a bystander is asked if he saw an old lady go by, the answer is: "I did not, but I saw a young girl, and she had the walk of a queen." Then the curtain falls on this short drama. We know that we are in the symbolist twilight zone, where vision is purely subjective, and time is the absolute and immutable moment. In *Baile's Strand* masks are used, as in Hofmannsthal's plays, thereby creating a greater remoteness around the fool and the blind.

Where Maeterlinck produced effective silences, Yeats suggests enigmatic atmosphere through the use of sounds, chants, and refrains in imitation of folklore. In his essay on "The Symbolism of Poetry," he said: "The theater began in ritual and it cannot come to its greatness again without recalling words to their ancient sovereignty." Whereas Mallarmé saw the power of words in the multiplicity of their meaning, Yeats goes after their auditory spell and probes their source of incantation. Thus in *Deirdre* we find the heroine recalling the memory of the spoken words:

I have heard terrible mysterious things
Magical horrors and spells of wizards [7]

The power of the refrain lies in its rhythm which, according to Yeats, prolongs the moment of contemplation.

Deirdre and *The Shadowy Waters* consummate Yeats' use of all these symbolist devices. Both plots are loosely woven, derived from Irish legend. Love operates in mysterious ways; with the intervention of

[7] The quotations from *Deirdre* and *The Shadowy Waters* used in this chapter are reprinted with permission of Mr. M. B. Yeats, Macmillan & Co. Ltd., and The Macmillan Company from *Collected Plays* by W. B. Yeats. Copyright 1934, 1952 by The Macmillan Company.

Druids and portentous birds, it creates a schism between the lovers and the rest of humanity, under the
vigilant eye of imminent and inevitable death.

Deirdre is a child-wife, much like Mélisande, found
and squired by an elderly King:

> Some Dozen years ago, King Conchubar found
> A house upon a hillside in this wood,
> And there a comely child with an old witch
> To nurse her, and there's nobody can say
> If she were human, or of those begot
> By an invisible king of the air in a storm
> Or a king's daughter, or anything at all
> Of who she was or why she was hidden there
> But that she'd too much beauty for good luck.

The encounter of true love is as implausible as it is
inevitable. The funereal grotto of the love tryst of
Pelléas and Mélisande is here replaced by the symbol
of a lethal chessboard, used by the couple "upon the
night they died." The premonition of death is the extra
dimension of the otherwise ordinary triangle; says
Deirdre to Naisi:

> When first we came into this empty house
> You had foreknowledge of our death. . . .

The Shadowy Waters, written first in 1900 as a poem
and rewritten several times between 1902 and 1906 to
bring it into dramatic focus, is the encounter of two
shipwrecks. One is the aimless voyage of Forgael, who
seeks communion with the Ever-living and is believed
by his sailors to be under the spell of the Druid and
endowed with a magic power to play the harp. In the
other ship sails a Queen, Dectora, whose husband has
been slain by her sailors. The fatality of their meeting
is likened to a "great golden net" that encircles them
and of which they shall be powerless to break a single
mesh. Eventually their sailors depart in Dectora's vessel

to enjoy the treasures they have found there; Forgael
and Dectora break the rope of their anchor, as if cut-
ting themselves off from a great umbilical cord, and
drift off to sea in a scene reminiscent of the communion in death of Axël and Sara, while their servants
are taking part in their wedding festivities. Forgael,
gathering about him Dectora's long hair, as powerfully
symbolic as Mélisande's locks, says:

> Beloved,
> having dragged the net about us,
> And knitted mesh to mesh, we grow immortal;
> And that old harp awakens of itself
> To cry aloud to the grey birds, and dreams,
> That have had dreams for father, live in us.

The portentous birds who hover over the characters
from the beginning of the play are described by the
sailors:

> Until the moon had set, and when I looked
> Where the dead drifted, I could see a bird
> Like a grey gull upon the breast of each.
> While I was looking they rose hurriedly,
> And often circling with strange cries awhile
> Flew westward; and many a time since then
> I've heard a rustling overhead in the wind.

The sea plays for Yeats the role that the forest assumed for Villiers and Maeterlinck: ageless, limitless,
abyssal, a source of magic:

> Where the world ends
> The mind is made unchanging, for it finds
> Miracle, ecstasy, the impossible hope,
> The flagstone under all, the fire of fires,
> The roots of the world.

The faithful sailor-servant, Aibric, warns Forgael, as
did Axël's confidant, that death lurks at the end of his

flirtations with dream existence. Forgael and Dectora convey their sense of limitless time by their ability to identify with the spirit of the legendary Aengus and Edaim:

> Is it not true
> That you were born a thousand years ago,
> In islands where the children of Aengus wind
> In happy dances under a windy moon,
> And that you'll bring me there?

The poem-play ends with the triumph of spiritual existence as the birds lead the couple off to "Ever-living land":

Where no child's born but to outlive the moon.

Yeats' plays were in a sense an illustration of his belief that Irish legends "may well give the opening century its most memorable symbols." The regeneration of these old symbols constituted for him the passing of a torch from the magicians of yore to those poets, musicians, and artists of his time who realized that they would learn their craft, not with pen and paper but through the exercise of imagination and its rich promises of transcendence: "How can the arts overcome the slow dying of men's hearts that we call the progress of the world, and lay their hands upon men's heartstrings again, without becoming the garment of religion as in old times?" It is to be noted that the difference between the artist mystic and the religious mystic is clearly defined when Yeats accords to the artist the "garment" of the materials of religion rather than the dogma or belief.

The correlation that is apparent between Yeats' essays on symbolism and his plays makes it obvious that his intention in art was not to produce theater in the dramatic sense of the word. There was no sense of frustration in his acceptance of the fact that his plays were unstageable. And the revisions that were eventually to make them more theatrically manageable, thanks to the Abbey Theater, did not to Yeats' mind enhance their quality. Edmund Wilson's view in *Axel's Castle* that "Yeats' plays have little dramatic import because Yeats himself had little sense of drama" needs to be revised in view of the theater's more recent attempts to view "theater" as something more than conversational chatter or the conflict of emotions. The recurrent efforts of ingenious directors and set-designers, who could create technical feats of lighting and décor attuned to the mood of the plays, have been able to bring back these plays from time to time as expressions of an "art theater." In this respect, symbolist theater has also received a strong shot in the arm from the pliability of advanced processes of photography, which can convey in the cinema illusions that are difficult to maintain on the stage.

The ingredients of symbolist theater, which germinated in Mallarmé's mind, materialized in plays from Maeterlinck to Yeats, have come to be viewed more and more as iconoclastic revisions of the notion of theater, rather than as weaknesses in dramatic composition. The so-called failures of the poet to transform the poem into theater have suggested to more recent artists the possibility of transforming theater into an oral poem. But the hard fact remains that symbolist theater cannot enjoy wide appreciation *as theater* until the notion of thematic communication is accepted as at least equal to that of consequential dialogue, or until spectators are willing and ready to consider the theater as a new temple of meditation and the play as the text of a new liturgy. Without oral rendition and audience participation in his work, the playwright remains a poet; and Yeats proves to be more realistic than Mallarmé when he terms his subjective dialogues "a different form of art."

VIII

THE AFTERGLOW

The fallacy in historical accounts of the Symbolist movement has been to measure its current in terms of "generations." From this point of view, symbolism would seem to be a ball tossed from one epoch to the other, until it disappears, uncaught, into a pit. This is the attitude suggested by Guy Michaud when he declares in *Message Poétique du symbolisme* that symbolism finally dies with the First World War. On the other hand, Edmund Wilson views symbolism along such broad lines in *Axel's Castle* that he is able to include the novels of Joyce and of Proust, the unintelligibilities of Gertrude Stein and the dadaists, under his broad definition, which says: "Symbolism may be defined as an attempt of carefully studied means—a complicated association of ideas represented by a medley of metaphors—to communicate unique personal feelings." [1]

The truth seems to lie between these two views. Symbolism in the twentieth century does not die so abruptly as suggested by Michaud, nor does it merge into other literary developments, such as the psychological novel, nor identify with other literary reactions and innovations such as dadaism and ensuing surrealism, which are endowed with a spirit of literary mutation quite alien to the *ars poetica* of symbolism. In fine, symbolism is not a heritage systematically handed down from one generation to the next—first,

[1] Edmund Wilson, *Axel's Castle* (New York: Scribner's, 1936), pp. 21–22.

because several generations were enriched by it simultaneously; second, because symbolism itself underwent drastic modifications with the passage of time. The years 1885–1890 were a time of converging action in Paris on the part of various nationals who worked together through the medium of the French language, and arrived at a theory, a technique, and a mystique to be henceforth associated with the notion of "symbolism." This was the period that we have regarded as the flowering of Symbolism with a capital "S," the stage of the literary school or *cénacle,* the convergence of poetic minds in Paris; and the French language was the common denominator of that poetic concept. By 1890, the outward action began, and the chief interest in symbolism, from the point of view of European rather than French literature, shifted to the consideration of what various poets of different nationalities took away from Paris and transposed into their own idiom. This was the epoch of Arthur Symons' translations of Baudelaire and Rimbaud, of literary criticism about symbolism in England, Italy and Germany —such as Vittorio Pica's *Letteratura d'eccezione* (1899) [2] and Stefan George's *Blätter für die Kunst*— and the crystallization of the literary conventions which become the earmarks of the symbolist mode of writing, as we have pointed out in a previous chapter. After 1900, as Michaud himself observes, there is the "prodigious extension" encompassing in the dissemination of symbolism, not only the countries of Western Europe, but of the east as well: Hungary, Rumania, Bulgaria, Greece, Poland. In Russia, the movement is abruptly aborted with the coming of the Revolution, whose premises were incompatible with a code of aesthetics in which the notion of an "elite," antago-

---

[2] Cf. Olga Ragusa, "French Symbolism in Italy," *The Romanic Review,* XLVI (October 1955) pp. 231–35 for guidelines and documented references concerning the spread of the symbolist convention in Italy.

nistic to mass communication, is so clearly inherent.

Actually, on the European rather than French scale, symbolism (now with a small "s") reaches its apogee around 1920, despite the advent of new movements which pull in opposite directions the literary talents of the new century. It is significant to note that the tremendous harvest of poetic writings of the early 1920's are all tinged with symbolist characteristics: Eliot's *The Waste Land,* Valéry's "Le Cimetière marin," and St. John Perse's *Anabasis* are all of 1922 vintage, as are Jiménez' *Segunda antología poética* and Ugo Betti's *Re Pensieroso;* Wallace Stevens' *Harmonium* and Rilke's *Duino Elegies* follow closely in 1923, Yeats' *The Wild Swans at Coole* (1919) and "Byzantium" (1933) cover a larger period. All these and many lesser works are affected by symbolism. In fact, the success and the large-scale ramification and popularization in poetic circles of the symbolist technique and spirit are made glaringly evident by the fact that every poet honored with the Nobel prize, from the time of Maeterlinck carries to a larger degree the character and conventions of symbolism than any other distinctive feature: Jiménez, St. John Perse, Quasimodo, Montale have this family trait. The hermetic character of symbolism became a universal code; which, if not directly understood, is easily recognized throughout the Western world as the standard poetic position in literature. In fact, symbolism became integrally associated with the poetic genre to such an extent that thereafter one had to take drastic, iconoclastic measures to introduce new poetic concepts, as the revolutionary character of the surrealist movement bears evidence.

Although, as we have seen, the theater form was able to effect more graphic and concrete implementation of symbolist theories than the poem, symbolism was not considered a *theatrical* success but an overflow of the poetic genre. Certainly, this is even more true of symbolism's connections with the novel form. If there are certain applications of symbolist attitudes in novels, such as the "decadent" spirit in Proust and in Thomas Mann's *Death in Venice,* the symbolist novel is a contradiction in terms, since the symbolist coterie abhorred the novel as it rejected all narrative forms; and if it may be possible to distinguish certain vestigial aspects of symbolist technique in the novel of the 1920's, there are too many other developments in the novel genre, quite alien to symbolism, which make it wiser for the critic to steer clear of that genre in appraising the repercussions of the symbolist movement. When we speak of symbolism, then—whether with a small or a capital "s," and either in its early stages or in the years of its spreading literary fortune—our basic substance is poetry; and it is in terms of poetry that the afterglow must be observed and identified.

The problem of identification can be handled from two different vantage points. In terms of generalities, we can ask ourselves how the various facets of symbolism have been affected or carried on through the years; in this respect, we can note modifications in the poetics or theories, in technique, and in the mystique. On the other hand, we can also appraise the extent to which certain major figures in European literature appropriated the common heritage of symbolism.

Proceeding from the first vantage point, what do we find in the works of the many diverse figures writing concurrently? The greatest degree of agreement appears to prevail in regard to the poetics of symbolism: the mission of the poet and his relations to his readers. The poet is not as isolated in the 1900's as in the years of the *fin de siècle,* but this does not mean that he has left the ivory tower. Rather, he seems to have admitted a certain percentage of the reading public into the tower. There is what we might call the poetization of the reader. In most of T. S. Eliot's comments about the effect of the poem, there is a definite awareness of the presence of the reader—and not simply a handful

of readers, such as the *habitués* of Mallarmé's Tues-
days. If there is hermeticism, for instance, there also
seems to be the foregone conclusion that this elliptic
writing must bring the reader—of course, the elite
reader—into some kind of communication with the
poet. Eliot says, in *The Uses of Poetry:* "meaning [is]
necessary to soothe the reader while the poem does its
work." Earlier symbolists would have been content
with whatever the poem had done to themselves; in
the process of creation here there is a definite intent
that the spirit of the poem permeate *the other* as well
as the self, in a relationship in which the reader becomes a kind of alter ego, or performs the function of
mirror for Narcissus. We see to what extent Eliot is
concerned with this intermediary importance of meaning, when we consider his voluminous explanatory
notes to *The Waste Land*. Orientation is in order, but
this does not mean downright explanation, which even
those neo-symbolists who want a reading public consider as anathema to the appreciation of poetry. We
find T. S. Eliot, despite his notes, objecting to the
practice in criticism which consists of "interpretation."
And in France L'Abbé Brémond chides the critic for
having used prosaic measures to "understand" poetry.
In his opinion, to explain a poem is to square the
circle; and when the enigma is gone, little remains to
challenge the elite reader.

Hermetic, cryptic, succinct in statement, the poet
wants, nevertheless, to a much higher degree than in
the earlier stages of symbolism, to establish an empathy with a certain category of reader. This awareness of the public on the part of the poet may be the
reason why the public has responded to symbolism in
the twentieth century, as it did not in the nineteenth.
On the other hand, the symbolist poet is far from re-
turning to the role of *bard*. He persists in considering
himself the *sage,* deriving his position from the definition of imagination given earlier by Baudelaire as the

highest quality of the intellect. To recall Baudelaire's letter to Toussenel in this connection: "I have been saying for a very long time that the poet is supremely intelligent, that he is intelligence itself, and that imagination is the most scientific of all faculties." In this same spirit we find Wallace Stevens many years later, in *The Language of Poetry,* qualifying as poet "any man of imagination."

As we have seen, a mistranslation of "esprit" in the last line of Baudelaire's "Correspondances": "les transports de l'esprit et des sens" confirmed for some of the early English theorists of symbolism the belief that Baudelaire had admitted the duality of the spirit and the flesh; on the contrary, Baudelaire's intention had really been to surrender poetry to the senses and to the *mind,* "l'intelligence illuminée par l'ivresse," as he explained in "Le Poème du haschisch." In the process of linking human sensations in their primary state with their intellectual transformations, there would not be much room left for the play of the emotions. The recipients of the symbolist legacy seem to have been clearly oriented in this direction: from Valéry to the Sitwells, poetry came to mean a series of intellectual strategies for the poet; and for the reader, an enigma calling upon his powers of insight. This notion of poetry as the supreme intellectual act enhances the hermetic character of symbolist orientation to such an extent that in Italy the words "hermeticism" and "symbolism" become in effect synonymous, and "difficult" becomes an attribute of the poet. Indeed, for Croce, poetry is a struggle of the mind against itself, a struggle against emotion, rising above human anguish, above right and wrong, above even the enjoyment of one's own suffering.

When the poet loads his poem with all sorts of literary and legendary allusions, it is often as bait to the reader, a teasing of his intellect rather than the conjuring of unusual images. This hermeticism is not in

line with the obscurities found in Mallarmé, which
guarded his intellectual privacy, but rather constitutes
a change or deviation from the symbolist notion of
the mission of the poet, who has now become conscious
of his audience and is interested in establishing a basis
for communication, even though the terms may be
forbidding. It is to be noted that in this kind of hermeticism, practiced by Eliot, Yeats, and the Italians,
the mystery of the poem can eventually be solved by
research or exegesis and is a conceit of the poet in
search of a particular audience rather than an act of
defiance and rejection of all audience, which the
sparsity of writing or the white page implied for
Mallarmé.

In this broadening of the aegis of symbolist poetics,
it should also be noticed that many poets accepting
the label of "symbolist" came to think of it as a more
general concept than had prevailed during the days of
the literary school. If the group of the 1880's associated
itself with Baudelaire and Schopenhauer as *a priori*
symbolists, now the ancestry is taken much further
back, to include Plato, Virgil, Dante, Góngora, and
others. As a result, many a poetic device is incorporated into "symbolist" poetry that is historically
alien to the possible influences of symbolism. This
fact looms openly in the case of T. S. Eliot as we shall
see a little later on.

In a previous chapter, we noted how certain conventions emerged from the technique of the early symbolists. Let us now see how these conventions evolved,
in the cross-fertilization that took place as symbolism,
spreading into literatures of varying traditions, mingled freely with these other influences in becoming a
naturalized citizen of countries other than France
where it was born.

As we have already seen, the symbolist technique re-
volved around the cult of the image and the new uses
of language intended to turn poetry from direct state-

ment of thought or emotion into indirect discourse, suggesting rather than stating the dream of the vision of the poet. How has this purpose and its implementation fared in the course of time?

Both T. S. Eliot and Wallace Stevens see the function of the image as the tideover in lieu of a direct statement of meaning between the poet and the beings with whom he wants to establish communication. "Genuine poetry can communicate before it is understood," says T. S. Eliot, and Wallace Stevens tells us, in *Notes Toward a Supreme Fiction,* that "the difficult rigor is forthwith on the image of what we see, to catch from that irrational moment its unreasoning." If with the early Symbolists the symbol conveys the ambiguous relation between the inner consciousness of man, the poet, and the physical world outside him, a new element—the communication of the relationship *to* that other—also comes into play, particularly as symbolism affects Anglo-Saxon poetry. On the other hand, T. S. Eliot also broadens the uses of the intermediary symbol when he defines the *objective correlative* as "a set of objects, a situation, a chain of events which shall be the formula of that *particular* emotion." [3] Emotion refers, of course, to the instigating vision of the poet rather than to a need for affective communication. Whereas, among the earlier symbolists the symbol had been concentrated almost exclusively on the object, now Eliot enlarges the scope of the intermediary symbol to include situations and thereby makes room for narration, which had previously been banished. With the reintroduction of narration, the equivocal character of the symbol becomes of course much more difficult to preserve.

Other factors are also working at this time against the ambiguity which we have heretofore considered a sina qua non of symbolist technique. We have seen

---

[3] T. S. Eliot, "Hamlet and His Problems," *The Sacred Wood* (2nd ed.; London: Methuen, 1928), p. 153.

that one way the symbol lost its ambiguity was through overuse, leading to specific identification. As a defense against spontaneous identification of overused symbols, some poets sought heretofore untapped myths for purposes of allusive evocation. Yeats was most successful in this search for new myths as he tapped richly and freely into Celtic legends, as we have already noted in his early dramatic verse. But where he caught by this means the magic of indirect communication, often the critic has stepped in and pulverized by exegesis the very quality that had made the multi-dimensional symbolist image something different from single-track allegory.

The symbol in latterday symbolism is constantly chased by the demon of allegory; the latter catches up with the symbol every time the symbol can be identified, either through previous usage or by critical clarification of its usage. Synesthesia is almost automatized in the regular coupling of the abstract with the concrete. The use of color to convey a unity of theme or of a mood continues, as we get the "Blue Guitar" of Stevens, the "Blancura" of Jorge Guillén, the "Sinfonía en gris mayor" of Rubén Darío, "Verde que te quiero verde" of Lorca, and too many others to warrant multiplication of examples. When the symbol itself finds it difficult to convey ambiguity, it is the image—consisting of several associated symbols—that is geared to express elliptic meaning. This is brought about in two opposite ways: through a distillation which makes the world outside become more rarefied and anemic, or an enrichment of detail, which makes it more sanguine, and in creating effects ends up by appealing to the sensuality rather than to the imagination of the reader. The former is the path of what has been called in France "pure" poetry as an outgrowth of symbolism; the latter gives us some of the sensual imagery of the Spanish and Latin American poets, as well as a certain hedonism in some Italian poets.

L'Abbé Brémond was the author of the notion of "pure poetry," which he had found in one of Valéry's writings, but which Valéry denied having any significance beyond the precisely applicable one in context. In this process of rarefaction of the image, all subject matter seemed to be banished as well as all descriptive detail that was capable of arousing emotions. The notion that poetry is the antithesis of the novel is here markedly brought out as it becomes evident that to teach, to tell a story, to paint, to move to emotion are all rejected from the sphere of the poem and relegated to the novel *genre*. In this sense, the evolution of symbolism in France made it almost impossible to write poetry; in effect, it reduced the poet to silence or to the white page, as was true of Valéry's twenty years of self-condemnation to silence, whereas the Anglo-Americans' more permissive turn to narration, like the Latins' indulgence in descriptive technique in the image, made it possible to have more prolific poetic expression in the spirit of symbolism, if not a totally orthodox adherence to its technique.

What happened to the symbolist notions of the music of poetry, as far as structure and function were concerned? T. S. Eliot understood Baudelaire's and Mallarmé's notions of the correspondence of music to poetry better than did the French technicians of the Symbolist school. In his article on "The Music of Poetry" he says: "The music of Verse is inseparable from the meanings and associations of words." This means that words are not to be used primarily for their onomatopoetic sounds, that the poet must find something more significant in the bewitchment of music than assonances and alliterations. He knows that the secret of music as an impulse to the imagination lies not in its sounds but in its power. In line with this, we find Eliot not particularly taken with the innovations in versification of the French instrumentalists, but drawn instead to the non-eloquence of Laforgue.

From him Eliot learns how to be poetic without being eloquent, how too much musicality of verse, instead of enhancing the poetic spirit, will distract the reader and break the spirit. He clearly defines in this light the frontiers of poetry: "Poetry may occur," he says in his preface to St. John Perse's *Anabasis,* "at any point along a line of which the formal limits are 'verse' and prose.' " [4] This means that verse in itself is not poetry, and that the truly prosaic does not consist simply in the elimination of verse, but that there is a wide margin—i.e. the field in which the modern poet must work —between the abandonment of regular prosody and that form of prose which is the tool of direct communication.

Again, there is a divergence of interpretation here between the Anglo-Saxons and the Latins. Spanish poetry of symbolist inspiration is much closer to the musicality of Verlaine and the Symbolist school of neumatic verse than to the concept of structural association launched by Baudelaire, nurtured by Mallarmé, and then taken up by T. S. Eliot, in theory, if not always achieved in practice. The French join the English here in espousing the more difficult objective, which in a sense proves unfeasible, and because of its difficulty of execution constantly threatens the poet with default. As Valéry says: "As a matter of fact, in authentic language the word has a function that consists not in representing, but in destroying. It makes things vanish. It produces the absence of the object; it nullifies it." Leaning away from eloquence, Eliot will lapse into private conversation, and Valéry into silence, whereas the Spaniards will sing and communicate on a broader scale.

All this leads us to the most important aspect of symbolism—its *mystique.* How diversified and altered does that aspect of symbolism become with the passage

[4] T. S. Eliot in Preface to St. John Perse, *Anabasis* (New York: Harcourt, Brace and World, 1949), p. 11.

of time? Michaud tells us that, whereas in the beginning the "decadent" spirit preceded and promoted symbolism, later it came to be dissociated from symbolism. This may be true to a certain extent with regard to French literature, which became invaded with other avant-garde movements and preserved symbolism more in its form than in its philosophy. But where the European extensions of symbolism are concerned there is to be found more variety and abandonment of the forms rather than of the philosophy connected with symbolism as we have defined it through the word "decadent" used in a specific connotation.

The great subject at the core of symbolism, as we have seen, was man's struggle against the void, as he visualized the power of death over consciousness. In all the important poets of the early twentieth century this strife persists as the dominant subject for which poetry is destined. In its range and variations we might call it *the dynamics of despair*. In addition, there is a continued awareness of the universal functions of the cult of Narcissus—the Universal Ego dealing with the single, eternal, persistent preoccupation of man, the only important problem of the human condition. Valéry expresses it beautifully when he says that "the highest power of contemplation of the mind is a form of narcissism that transcends egotism." Concern with self becomes the means of preserving what is human in the cosmic void. Most of the great vein of cosmic poetry prevalent under the guise of symbolism is a defense of the human element in the midst of the abyss, rather than the admiration of the cosmic which occurs when the cosmic is taken as the creation of God. Like Maeterlinck, Unamuno calls death the intruder, designates it as "Aquélla"—that one over there—so different in character from the human whom it is intent on destroying.

Our defense against the enemy is through refuge in the dream and through faith in that absurd illusion

which is life. Time is still considered the assistant of
the adversary and is therefore pictured as "cruel," for
with time death will always prove the winner, even
where the human may find temporary surcease. The
soul, then, becomes an earthly product in this form of
mysticism, which recognizes the abyss not as a future
hell or a paradise, but as the oblivion of human consciousness. "Decadent" in this sense is not involved
with questions of morality: it is neither right nor
wrong that we die, and our acts, good or bad, will not
change the situation. To be a poet is simply to be more
highly aware of the spiritual crisis in which we are involved with our every breath, and to express all else
in the light of that single, significant truth. Our temporary refuges are the dream and involvement in the
work of art.

Jacques Maritain in his *Notes on Modern Poetry* observes that in the end the poet will find himself in a
void and discover that the refuge he has sought for
in his spirit led him to "the most flimsy forms, in fact
. . . nothingness and in silence"; he would, therefore,
be compelled to return to religion, to rediscover God,
if not for the sake of his soul, then at least in order
to rescue his art from a state of attrition. This is in
fact what happened with T. S. Eliot and Paul Claudel
in their eventual religious conversion; in their case,
symbolism led in effect, from descent back to ascen-
sion.

However, in propagating the "decadent" spirit, there
emerged an aesthetic as well as a spiritual problem.
What happens when the *mystique* overpowers the
purely artistic concern of the poet? Whether the *mystique* evolves into religious revival, as metaphysical
verse, in the English sense of the word, or remains
agnostic but still "metaphysical," in the French sense
of the word (where it means simply *any* awareness of
man's spiritual plight), symbolism lies in danger of
turning into philosophical verse. In other words, the

poet fails to channel the curse of being mortal into an art image, but expresses it in terms of the personal ego; the result is not the poetic alchemy of symbolism, but philosophy set to verse. This proved a poets' pitfall for many symbolists, particularly among the Germans.

The problem is treated in Eliot's article on Dante in *The Sacred Wood*. He disagrees with Valéry, who had suggested that modern man cannot accept philosophical verse. Admitting that "The original form of philosophy cannot be poetic," Eliot suggested that it is perhaps our handling of philosophy that is amiss, rather than philosophic poetry such as Dante's. If philosophy in its initial stage is something perceived, it should not be introduced in its bare form into poetry. Eliot's definition of philosophy is, in fact, "something perceived." According to him, if modern poets are not successful with philosophical verse, the fault does not lie with philosophical verse but with their own shallow resources: "When most of our modern poets confine themselves to what they have perceived, they produce for us, usually, only odds and ends of still life and stage properties, but that does not imply so much that the method of Dante is obsolete as that our vision is perhaps comparatively restricted." [5]

Between the danger of no philosophy at all and totally overt philosophy, Eliot therefore suggests a compromise, a philosophical modification, which is not what the poet has digested into abstractions but which, as the words of an oracle, has philosophical meaning that is subject to many interpretations; the multiplicity of possible meaning is the secret of the universality of such poetry. Even as the mission and position of the poet was characterized, as we have seen, by awareness of the presence of the reader, so the definition which Eliot suggests for the expression of philosophic intent assumes a recipient. There may be much more in a

[5] T. S. Eliot, "Dante," *The Sacred Wood, op. cit.*, pp. 162–71.

poem than the author is aware of. The differences in
interpretations indicate that "the poem means more,
not less, than ordinary speech can communicate,"
Eliot tells us in the article "The Music of Poetry."
The differences between philosophical verse and this
philosophical modification is clearly illustrated in the
difference between two poems of Wallace Stevens, both
of which appear in *Harmonium*. They show succinctly
why in Anglo-American poetry a distinction is made
between symbolic and metaphysical verse, whereas
such an antithesis has no place in French poetry. In
the two poems, the subject is the same: the search for
a foothold, as it were, in the abyss surrounding
human life. In the first passage, from "Negation," this
question is treated as a philosophical subject, in direct
expression, communicating through abstract nouns
and simple statements the ideas that arise from the
poet's nihilistic state of mind, which may be considered akin to the moods we have seen among symbolists; but so involved is the poet in the ideas that
there is nothing of the form or technique of symbolism:

Hi! The creator is blind,
Struggling toward his harmonious whole,
Rejecting intermediate parts
Horrors and falsities and wrongs;
Incapable master of all force,
Too vague idealist, overwhelmed
By an afflatus that persists.
For this, then, we endure brief lives,
The evanescent symmetries
From that meticulous potter's thumb.[6]

On the other hand, the second passage, from "Curtains
in the House of the Metaphysician," has the ellipticity

6 The quotations from Stevens' works used in this chapter are
reprinted from *Collected Poems of Wallace Stevens* by permission
of Alfred A. Knopf, Inc. Copyright 1923 and renewed 1951 by
Wallace Stevens.

or symbolism in succinct images suggesting the solitude, the silence, the vertigo of man before the abyss that engulfs him—but in terms of things he can perceive rather than just think about:

It comes about that the drifting of these curtains
Is full of long motions; as the ponderous
Deflations of distance; or as clouds
Inseparable from their afternoons;
Or the changing of light, the dropping
Of the silence, wide sleep and solitude
Of night, in which all motion
Is beyond us, as the firmament,
Up-rising and down-falling, bares
The last largeness, bold to see.

Do we then have a working yardstick with which to measure the symbolism of certain of the great figures of modern poetry, a method of observation other than "interpretation" or historical narration in the critical study of poetry? To start with in the passages just quoted from Wallace Stevens, it is obvious that for him "symbolist" is one of several manners possible to assume in writing poetry, rather than a total commitment, although some of his pronouncements about poetry closely approximate symbolist poetics. What of other poets whose generalizations we have cited?

Yeats' "Leda and the Swan" is a symbolist masterpiece constructed in the very spirit of Mallarmé's understanding of symbolist technique. His use of the myth of the rape of Leda by Zeus disguised as a swan has the same type of creative originality as Mallarmé's handling of such tired myths as those associated with Pan and Salome. Mallarmé had suggested that the poet, in writing about a storm that strikes a forest, must describe neither the thunder nor the forest, but the effect of the one on the other. This is exactly what Yeats achieves in the short but densely meaningful poem when he designates neither the swan nor the girl but the effect of the blow of the swan on the girl: "staggering girl," "thighs caressed by . . . dark webs," "shudder in the loins," rather than stating the rape he suggests the sudden, unexpected sexual act in symbolist imagery: "terrified . . . fingers push the feathered glory from her loosening thighs."

A sudden blow: the great wings beating still
Above the staggering girl, her thighs caressed
By the dark webs, her nape caught in his bill,
He holds her helpless breast upon his breast.

How can those terrified vague fingers push
The feathered glory from her loosening thighs?
And how can body, laid in that white rush,
But feel the strange heart beating where it lies?

A shudder in the loins engenders there
The broken wall, the burning roof and tower
And Agamemnon dead.
                              Being so caught up,
So mastered by the brute blood of the air,
Did she put on his knowledge with his power
Before the indifferent beak could let her drop? [7]

As symbol replaces direct narrative statement, Yeats implies, by means of a few images, the consequences of the conception that occurs: Leda, who becomes the mother of Castor and Pollux and of Helen of Troy, in that slight moment of her encounter with Zeus predetermines the fate of a civilization:

A shudder in the loins engenders there
The broken wall, the burning roof and tower
And Agamemnon dead.

The symbolist technique of focusing on the part rather than the whole shows us the contrast, physically and

[7] Reprinted with permission of Mr. M. B. Yeats, Macmillan & Co. Ltd., and The Macmillan Company from *The Collected Poems of W. B. Yeats.* Copyright 1928 by The Macmillan Company, renewed 1956 by Georgie Yeats.

spiritually between the god and the girl; he is the knowledge and the power behind the "great wings," "feathered glory," "brute blood," and "indifferent beak;" she is "staggering" and passive as she becomes a "thigh," a "helpless breast," a "nape" and "terrified . . . fingers."

In the confrontation of Leda and the swan Yeats achieved the double feat of evoking the Greek legend and expressing all the melding of physical and spiritual factors in the human embrace: the wonder, the terror, and the abyss of the unseen and unpredictable, as so much ensues from so short a moment. Never were so few words so telling about man's condition and his precarious destiny.

"Leda" dates from 1923. In a later period instances of purely symbolist poems are harder to detect. As "Byzantium" assumes the notion of "decadence," we note one of the most beautiful and powerful examples of the survival of the symbolist self-contained image. Here two manners of communication are combined— the direct, conceptual expression and the subjective impression of the fall of the Empire are climaxed in the last two stanzas by what Yeats himself calls:

Those images that yet
Fresh images beget [8]

He reaches the summit of the poem with the final one:

That dolphin-torn, that gong-tormented sea.

How does T. S. Eliot fare as a symbolist poet? Although he has himself acknowledged his affinity with symbolism, particularly with Laforgue, in Eliot's work, as in Stevens', symbolism appears to be *one of many manners.* In his case, this is not a vacillation—symbolism marks a stage in his development as a man of letters, after which a definite break occurs in the direction he takes. Although he suggests that the influences of Laforgue and the metaphysical poets of seventeenth-century England are concurrent influences on him. They seem to have operated, in effect, a conflict in him, and the metaphysical wins out in the end over the symbolist. *The Waste Land* and the *First Quartet* show a style as divergent from the later works as in the case of a painter a rose period from a blue period.

We know that T. S. Eliot was introduced to symbolist aesthetics through his contacts with Arthur Symons, and we also know that he admired not only Laforgue but also Baudelaire, Verlaine, and Mallarmé. But you are not always influenced by what you admire, and admission of influence is not always proof of influence. The best of critics is a poor self-critic at best, if he is a critic at all of his own work. The only valid judgment is one based on internal evidence. But in referring to the work itself, it is imperative to keep in mind *what else* may have helped shape it. In reading the early works of Eliot, where the possibility of symbolist influence is most probable, we must bear in mind that those were also the years in which he had been reading John Donne and the newly, posthumously published poems of Gerard Manley Hopkins. The "metaphysical" images of Donne also illustrate ideas, as does the symbol; but here there is definite *a priori* subject matter, there is descriptive language, there is specific allegory. Points made metaphorically are reinforced logistically. The cult of the image to reinforce abstractions in Eliot's poetry could derive just as easily from Donne as from the symbolists. As for the ellipsis of language which, as we have seen, assists the symbolist poet in establishing the ambiguous character of the image, Gerard Manley Hopkins has used the same device in a more urbane, colloquial way.

The colloquial language of Laforgue is never obscure; what makes Hopkins' style distinctive is the fact that he seems to speak the language of every man but with the power to pun inherent in the sophisticated mind. In that sense, Eliot is much closer to Hopkins than to Laforgue. The apparent colloquialism of Hopkins seems to have been inspired by a love of words, the sound of words that spontaneously conjure each other in rapid succession, arranging themselves into a direct statement, as in "The Windhover":

> No wonder of it: sheer plod makes plough down sillion
> Shine, and blue-beak embers, ah my dear,
> Fall, gall themselves, and gash gold-vermillion.[9]

The spirit of this imagery is far from being nihilistic; the azure decked in its metaphors does not lead to a fear of the abyss, but serves as a signal to the glory of the Maker. This is what the poem "Hurrahing in Harvest" with its verbal ambiguities, leads to:

> And the azurous hung hills are his world-wielding shoulder
> Majestic—as a stallion stalwart, very-violet-sweet!—
> These things, these things were here and but the beholder
> Wanting; which two when they once meet,
> The heart rears wings bold and bolder
> And hurls for him, O half hurls earth for him off
> under his feet.

Thus Hopkins illustrates perfectly what Eliot meant by the concept of philosophical modification; with him, the objective correlative comes through as objects ("azurous hung hills," "a stallion," etc.), a situation (man beholding the wonders of Creation), and a chain

---

[9] The quotations from the works of Hopkins used in this chapter are from *Poems of Gerard Manley Hopkins,* Third Edition, edited by W. H. Gardner. Copyright 1948 by Oxford University Press, Inc. Reprinted by permission.

of events (the narration that informs the reader first of things that exist, then of the relations between these things and the beholder). The ellipses of words produce very little ellipsis of thought, as they do in the most authentically symbolist poems. But Hopkins indicated to Eliot how to be intellectually elliptical, to exercise the supreme prerogative of the poet to use language in a private way and still to convey the philosophical thought. These are the characteristics that prevail throughout the works of Eliot, whereas the "decadent" spirit evident in his earliest poems—and which he owes to symbolism more than to anything else—is later abandoned for religious transcendence. With the example of Hopkins before him, he could readily assume this, without having to change his style in any drastic fashion; for Hopkins has demonstrated magnificently that you can be ambiguous and elliptical and pursue symbols and images, without nursing a nihilistic, escapist philosophy.

In examining the works of T. S. Eliot from the point of view of symbolism, in the first score of years of the twentieth century in which the literary fortune of symbolism is in its ascendency, what do we find truly to have its source in the symbolist spirit and aesthetics, as opposed to those trends which might better be identified with purely British sources?

There are states of mind associated with color, such as the yellow fog in "The Love Song of J. Alfred Prufrock"; there are frequent couplings of the abstract with the concrete such as in *Preludes:*

his soul stretched tight across the skies
That fade behind a city block

or in *The Waste Land:*

I will show you fear in a handful of dust.

There is animistic transfer of mood to things inanimate, as in

> the grass is singing
> Over the tumbled graves [10]

In *The Waste Land* particularly we can recognize the arid landscape, rarefied, emptied of living pulse and movement, with which we have become familiarized in symbolist poetry. The great "decadent" themes derived from the mortality of man: age, death, fear of living, the sterility of man's endeavors, the void—represented by Eliot in the expanses of the waste land. Wilson has chided Eliot for having called himself "old" in "Prufrock" when he was barely forty; but is this not truly a case where the universal psyche was transcending the personal self, and Eliot was contemplating the "daily tragic" factor of the universal aging process? This was the Orphic "self's" complaint, rather than that of a man of forty bemoaning his particular fate.

Lest in specifying the attitudes that link Eliot with the symbolists I should identify him integrally with them, let me hasten to observe that much of this spirit is conveyed in terms that are remote from the aesthetics of symbolism. He is most truly symbolist in the first four lines of *The Waste Land,* so effective in their power to blend the physical image of putrefaction with the mood of attrition and isolation of the poet; thereafter, the manner changes and is not resumed until the first three lines of "The Fire Sermon," as an echo of the prelude. But between the momentarily symbolistic evidences in *The Waste Land,* as elsewhere, there are other forces that pull Eliot toward procedures that are quite alien to symbolism. First is the narrative and

[10] T. S. Eliot, *Preludes* and *The Waste Land, Collected Poems 1909–1962* (New York: Harcourt, Brace and World, 1963). Reprinted by permission of the publishers, Harcourt, Brace and World and Faber and Faber, Ltd.

descriptive manner, which he seems to be incapable of abandoning. Then there is the cult of the image for its own sake, rather than as a means of stressing relationships between the inner and the outer world of the artist. This is particularly true in the *Preludes*. Have we ever seen a symbolist poet attracted by anything so earthly as the smell of steak? There are, above all, the obscurities which are there not to evoke unnameable intellectual states, as in Mallarmé, but which are easily decipherable and can be reduced to logical comprehension, as can be evidenced by all the clever explanations that Eliot's critics, guided by his notes, have been able to give in identifying the remotest of his symbols. This was certainly not in the spirit of the symbolist aesthetics; it is much closer to the verbal strategies of Hopkins, and intended for intellectual elucidation rather than spiritual illumination.

Although Eliot spoke often of his soul, the word "self" can easily be substituted in each instance, a self that is urbane and, let us admit it, often pedestrian. If Eliot has dreamed, he does not give much evidence of it in his poetry. A world that is sterile and empty is poignant only by contrast with a soul that is rich and teeming; otherwise, it is simply dull. Unless you are intent on working out a critical cross-word puzzle, Eliot can be terribly tedious; he possesses to a very minor degree the power to set you dreaming, which was the primary purpose of poetry as conceived by the symbolists. In Eliot's verse, the vision is either intellectually suggestive or sensually self-evident; the obscurities are almost never conducive to imaginative speculation, but merely to intellectual clarification. You don't want to muse with him, you have a strong desire to decipher him. His work leads to criticism in that sense, and, as we know, his critics have been many. But once everything has been explained, what then will remain of Eliot's place in symbolism?

It becomes almost inevitable to conclude that his

contribution to the lineage of symbolism was in the prestige he succeeded in giving to the poet as a man of intellect, as the supreme perceiver, rather than in terms of any further perfecting of the symbolist aesthetics. As the relations with the symbolists fade into his past, Eliot's powers of philosophical modification seem also to diminish; direct discourse, almost imageless, abstract in its word structure, is characteristic of the last three *Quartets,* by contrast with the first. Since the thought thus expressed is not particularly original, one wonders how it would have fared had the "illusion" of poetry been dispelled, and the sentences simply been strung end to end. The danger of philosophical "verse" is that, unless it has value as "verse," it is unlikely that it will stand up on its merits as "philosophy."

The final alienation of Eliot from the symbolist frame of reference occurs when he becomes a convert to Anglo-Catholicism, thereby becoming separated from the symbolist agnosticism as well as from its aesthetics. Indeed, in the long view, he looms much more important as a symbolist critic than as a symbolist poet.

◉

Among the German poets of the epoch, Rilke perhaps best suggests the proximity to symbolism. His period of greatest contact with the symbolist climate was between 1899 and 1902; he was introduced to symbolism through intermediaries, as was the case with T. S. Eliot. In this instance, the links were Stefan George, whom he met in 1897, and his reading of Maeterlinck's works. In 1899 he saw *Pelléas et Mélisande* performed in Berlin, and he himself staged a performance of *Soeur Béatrice,* another of Maeterlinck's plays. The two characteristics of the typical symbolist that Rilke possesses, and which were alien to Eliot, are the interplay of the dream with reality, and the sense of the "gouffre." Like Verlaine or Mallarmé, he is at home in that ineffable world between reality and the dream. The German words alliterate in mystical convergence; for example:

Ich bin zu Hause zwischen Tag und Traum

In Rilke's definition of the "soul," there is evidence of the symbolist mystique: "man probably begins where we think that he ends; where his visible life ends, there lies the beginning of the life of his soul, which is the only true life." There is no smell of steak in this purified notion of existence, which is an ever-rebellious rejection of the flesh and the mortal fragility to which the flesh is subjected. He gives us a definition of the "gouffre" quite as vertiginous as Baudelaire's and Mallarmé's; in an interrogation of his soul he says: "Du bist noch nicht Kalt, und es ist nicht zu spät in deine werdinden Tiefen zu tauchen, wo sich das Leben ruhig verrät." He loves silences, as did Maeterlinck. Death is again represented in his imagery as the intruder, waiting for its prey:

Der Tod ist gross
Wir sind die Seinen
Lachenden Munds
Wenn wir uns mitten im Leben meinen
Wagt erzu weinen
mitten in uns [1]

If, in all his poems, Rilke had used the simple explanatory style evident in the above passage, the same criticism could be made of him as of Eliot. But much more often the mood, which conveys man's constant crisis between life and death, between the dream escape and the fearful exposure to the realities of life, is embodied by Rilke in images of doors, castles, corridors, fountains; these possess, as Baudelaire said in "Correspondances," "the expansion of infinite things,"

[1] "Schluszstück," *Das Buch der Bilder*, Book II, Part I.

rather than being subject to identification, as was the case with Eliot.

Der Gedanke
Dass die Fontäne allein
draussen im Garten in Mondenschein
Ihre Wasser warf
war wie eine Welt [1]

In his dramatic works Rilke, like Hofmannsthal vacillated between symbolism and naturalism, the link being again the fatalistic pessimism perpetrated by man's plight, as he is battered by the universe. In the *White Princess,* which is characteristic, we find a young woman who remains virgin with her old husband while she awaits her lover for eleven years. Fate—here represented by the missing of signals—foils the long-awaited meeting. The environment in which the tale unfolds is very reminiscent of Maeterlinck: a palace near the sea, human figures absorbed into the fog of sunset, an old park full of mysterious shadows. In another play, *Das tägliche Leben* (Daily Life), we find the disproportion between measured time and the subjective intensity that humans can give to it. George and Helen meet for two hours, and it is a lifetime; they illustrate dramatically the symbolist notion of life considered as a daily crisis. Although, as in the case of Eliot, Rilke in his *Duino Elegies* falls time and again into the non-symbolist manner of philosophical verbalization, he appears to retain to a much greater extent the mystique of symbolism, suggesting an un-interrupted flow between the self that generates a current and the verbal transformation that occurs; the symbol is the mirror of the self rather than its adornment.

◉

The hermeticism apparent in Italian poetry of the symbolist vein is often due to the character of the

[1] "Die aus dem Hause Colonna," *Das Buch der Bilder,* Book II, Part I.

Italian language itself; it effects a compact expression
froth with meaning, which in other languages has to
be sought through contrived ambiguities in the creation of the image. Examples of such succinct verse are
found in Ungaretti's "Mattina:"

M'illumino
d'immenso

and in Quasimodo's equivocal use of the word
"Spazio" to convey simultaneously the image of time
and space:

Uguale raggio mi chiude
in un centro di buio,
ed è vano ch'io evada.
Talvolta un bambino vi canta
non mio; breve è lo spazio
e d'angeli morti sorride.

Mi rompe. Ed è amore alla terra
ch'è buona se pure vi rombano abissi
di acque, di stelle, di luce;
se pure aspetta, deserto paradiso,
il suo dio d'anima e di pietra.

But unlike conjunctions between single words, the
structure of the image itself often fails to suggest the
type of multiplicity of meaning found in Mallarmé
and perpetuated by Valéry. In Quasimodo, the correspondences between nature and the state of the soul
are often self-evident, as in the following piece from
Oboe sommerso (The Sunken Oboe):

in me si fa sera;
l'acqua tramonta
sulle mie mani erbose.

Ali oscillano in fioco cielo,
làbili: il cuore trasmigra
ed io son gerbido,

e i giorni una maceria.

The symbols often fall into simple allegory, as in
Ungaretti's "I fiumi" where the poet identifies the
stages of his life with rivers and flowers at the end of
the poem:

Questi sono i miei fiumi
contati nell' Isonzo

Questa è la mia nostalgia
che in ognuno
mi traspare
ora ch'è notte
che la mia vita mi pare
uno corolla
di tenebre

And in the final stanza of "O Notte," from Ungaretti's
Vita d'un Uomo, the barren elements correspond to
the inner sterilities, in the Laforgue manner:

Oceanici silenzi,
Astrali nidi d'illusione,
O notte.

The lyricism of its simple melancholy has the appeal
and communicative power of Verlaine's *Fêtes galantes*
and *Romances sans paroles.* Indeed admiration and
imitation of Verlaine persisted in the Latin countries
as violins continued to weep, winds sigh, and old parks
dream of their bitter sweet memories. Such is the
lament in "Parque viejo," from Jiménez's *Rimas de
sombra:*

Me he asomado por la verja
del viejo parque desierto:
todo parece sumido
en un nostálgico sueño.

Jimenez's park, less barren than Verlaine's in "Colloque sentimental," conveys at the end the same sense
of futility and quiet resignation:

El jardín vuelve a sumirse
en melancólico sueño,
y un ruiseñor, dulce y alto,
gime en el hondo silencio.

In Spanish literature, Lorca holds a position much like that of Baudelaire in French. Many trends converge to compose this complex poetry. For Lorca, symbolism is much like what Romanticism was for Baudelaire—a strong base, a spring-board. But it is a striking testimony to the broad aegis of symbolism that the movement could bring an elemental poetic spirit such as Lorca within its orbit, as well as supreme intellectuals such as Eliot or Valéry. Lorca is symbolist primarily in the same sense as we have seen Verlaine to be symbolistic. His verse is sung before it is comprehended; music comes before meaning in its neumatic rather than structural character. He uses all the flexibility of verse forms and word alliances to make poetry almost independent of word meaning—"romanceros," like Verlaine's "romances," but richer in melodies, more haunting, more earthy.

Lorca has the power to turn the sensual into the mystical to a degree that has not been observed since Baudelaire. Whereas in Eliot's sensual images there is no transcendence, Lorca injects into his seas, suns, stars, moons, olive fields, orange groves, trees, a morbidity that echoes the anguish which he, Lorca, calls the "duende." This is an almost untranslatable word that combines, one might say, the sense of "ennui," the anguish of "gouffre," and the sigh of futility. In commenting on Falla's "Nights in the Gardens of Spain" Lorca said: "Everything has black sounds, like the *duende.*" It seems to be the perfect translation. No one has appropriated the color synesthesia indicated in Rimbaud's "Voyelles" in quite as total a manner as Lorca: blue rose, green wind, red of blood and violence. But if the red is too often allegoric in its precision, the other colors make such irrational symbols that they bring Lorca midway toward surrealism; and, indeed, in his poetry the two movements intermingle, as in Baudelaire symbolism intercepted and evolved the Romantic technique. The following poem from *Romancero gitano* is an example of the use of the color green and the various forms of synesthesia it provokes in the poet:

Verde que te quiero verde.
Verde viento. Verdes ramas,
El barco sobre la mar
y el caballo en la montaña,
con la sombra en la cintura
ella sueña en su baranda,
verde carne, pelo verde,
con ojos de fría plata.
Verde que te quiero verde.
Bajo la luna gitana,
las cosas la están mirando
y ella no puede mirarlas.

The power of true symbolist technique looms in most dazzling fashion in those poems where Lorca desists from the temptations of narration and proves capable of the symbolist *tour de force*—of using his ample subject matter as images in series, rather than as an account of actions and events, thus truly transforming events into legends.

The intermingling of the abstract and the concrete, which we have noted so often in symbolist style, undergoes a state of evolution in Lorca, as Lorca avoids the pitfalls of allegory by making the connection between these two levels of perception a disconnected or irrational alliance; thus he bridges the gulf between symbolism and surrealism as few poets have done in our time. The other tremendous quality of his art is his unique ability to turn the regional into the universal. Most symbolist poets achieved universality of symbol

by referring to a non-national, common pool of mythology, such as the Greek, and stylizing these symbols
until they became quite as abstract as numerical figures. Lorca digs deep into the Spanish, as Yeats into
the Celtic; but where it is the vagueness of his reference that saved Yeats from descriptive regionalism, it
is through his music, and through the elemental common denominators, which Lorca succeeds in channeling from the particular to the general, that he man-
ages to transcend the Spanish subject, even as his
vision transcends all subject through the rhythm and
color of its landscapes in the suggestive power of his
"amarga" and tragic sense of life.

⊙

Finally, in France itself, symbolism reaches its apogee in Valéry and its denouement in St. John Perse.
It is Paul Valéry who seems to have adhered most
closely to Eliot's notion that philosophy must undergo
modification if it is to be of service to the poet. Basically, "Le Cimetière marin," written in the same year
as *The Waste Land,* treats the same "subject"—except
that the word "subject" has a derogatory sense where
symbolism is concerned. Let us say, rather, that its
philosophical concern is the same as that of *The Waste
Land:* the cemetery as indicative of attrition and of
the futility of human endeavor as the waste spaces of
Eliot's landscape. But few are the abstractions that
Valéry employs in the transmission of the fear, the
regrets, and the resignation, which are in effect an
interplay of theme and variations in the Mallarméan
use of musical structure.

Here the techniques of Rimbaud are combined with
those of Verlaine, as the general connotation (Verlaine) is interspersed with specific delimitations of
vision (Rimbaud); and thus banal notions avoid stereotyped forms. The oblique allusion directs the thought,
rather than embodies it. The purpose of the obscurity

is not simply an invitation to the reader to decipher its meaning, but rather to open various, often divergent avenues to thought. If there are a few conceits reminiscent of Eliot in the references such as Zeno of Elea, Hydra, Achilles, they are very minor factors in the ambiguity of the poem. All explanations of Valéry —there are as many of "Le Cimetière marin" as there are of *The Waste Land*—are arbitrary, because the secret of the obscurity is not one of hidden source but of structural ellipsis, of the elimination of explanatory words. There is, as a result, nothing as incompatible with the spirit of the poem as the explanations of editors, and as that photograph of the cemetery of Sète, with which all similarities are coincidental in terms of *poetic reality*. How can anything be explained, when each image serves as a spring-board for innumerable other invisible images?

While Mallarmé declared that to name an object was to rob it of three-quarters of its charm, Valéry discovered that to name an object in relation to others, but without defining the relationship, in effect charged the object with infinitely more meaning. Valéry, like Eliot, was an intellectual before all else; but whereas the work of art serves as a foil to Eliot, and Eliot looms greater than his work of art, Valéry is constantly making himself subservient to the work, his intellect becoming the humble servant of the work of art. There is no irregularity of verse or modification of prosody in Valéry's poem; he understands music, even as Baudelaire and Mallarmé, as a form of superior thinking, not sounds to be merely enjoyed, but in one of the unique coincidences in the history of poetry, Valéry's outer ear is in deep harmony with the inner ear, and the structure and musicality contribute almost equally to the rendition of the poem.

The coupling of the abstract with the concrete never achieved as delicate an interrelationship between the inner landscape and the exterior objects as in "Le

Cimetière marin." In the first stanza, the verb "pal-
pite" is caught among so many nouns that its application is ambiguous: since neither roofs nor high noon
can be said to "palpitate," this is really a simulation
of the poet's heartbeat projected on the objects. When
the sun is said to repose on the abyss, we are not sure
whether it is the physical "gouffre" of the sea, or the
sense of abyss conveyed in the poet by the cemetery, or
the bowels of the earth, suggested by the physical
reality of a cemetery. Any one of these choices would
be wrong, the simultaneous grasp of many meanings
would be the only true and total grasp of the picture,
the ambiguity being an integral part of the symbol.

A little later, the subjective silence of the poet is
identified with the objective silence of the place, and
the relationship abridged into a symbol, "Edifice dans
l'âme," which marks the conjunction of the imperceptible "âme" (soul) with the perceptible "édifice,"
both partaking of the physical and metaphysical "silence." When we come to the lines:

La scintillation sereine sème
Sur l'altitude un dédain souverain.

we have that miracle of total coincidence of all the
characteristics of symbolism that we have been trying
to distinguish in this study. There is the music, in both
senses of the word: the bewitching sound picture conjured by the s-sound, and at the same time the sum-
ming up, like a chord, of several concepts already introduced—such as palpitation, silence, abyss—all of
them comprehended at once. Just so, in hearing a
chord, you have neither the conscious spelling out of
the notes that compose it nor the verbalization of a
specific concept. We also find the interlocking of several sense-perceptions in the synesthesia of light and
sound; the coupling of the physical act of sowing with
the abstract quality of disdain; and, finally, the "deca-

dent" spirit that propels the image suggesting the depth of anguish before the indifference of the universe. The symbol is ambiguous, conducive to a state of mind, and indicative of the agnostic attitude which we have been able to determine in the long line of kindred spirits who have used symbolism as a process of somber meditation.

Later in the poem's progression into the various aspects of the notion of "void," we come upon:

Amère, sombre et sonore citerne,
Sonnant dans l'âme un creux toujours futur!

Here the "amarga," or spiritual connotation attributed to the object "citerne," implies physical depth, when it is taken in conjunction with subjective abyss; and "sombre" and "sonore" duplicate their alliterative association in the intermingling of the visual and the sound image. In both cases, they negate their usual qualities, and the implication of this rejection confirms the spiritual darkness of the poet's state of mind. The line:

Où tant de marbre est tremblant sur tant d'ombres;

suggests the infinite and inexpressible struggle of matter over spirit; but no verbalization will equal the impact or approximate the meaning of the symbol created by that particular juxtaposition of the abstract and the concrete. As we continue in the galaxy of images, that are never unilateral but with every statement refer at the same time to the material decomposition and the mental oblivion, we are reminded how banal the theme is, how totally it has already been treated by Thomas Gray and other elegiac poets.

We marvel then that such a meager, abused vein of "subject" matter can unleash such a complexity of metaphoric pattern—the concrete generalities: the roof, the worm, the fire, the sea; the Hamletlike morbidity, reminiscent of Laforgue:

Ce crâne vide et ce rire éternel!

the soul's earthbound quality expressed through the
Universal Ego:

Je hume ici ma future fumée,

and that most devastating of images, which sums up
the whole grim cycle of creation, fatal and redeeming
at once:

L'argile rouge a bu la blanche espèce,
Le don de vivre a passé dans les fleurs!

Unquestionably, the theme of death so prevalent in
the nineteenth century lingers at the core of the symbolist heritage, even though near the end of his poem,
Valéry resolves the nihilism into a determined stoicism:

Le vent se lève! . . . Il faut tenter de vivre!

The rhythm changes, and in a breaking action the
dreamy, somber meditation is dissipated, as if the bitterness might be washed away with the waves, even as
the banishment of the thought alone can make it possible to carry on the process of living. And with the
reference to the roof we are back to the beginning of
the poem, as in the composition of a musical work,
the last chord resolving the first.

We might say that much of St. John Perse consists
of variations on themes proposed in this rich, dense
poem of Valéry. Each of the images serves as a title
for Perse: "Amers," "Vents," the sea images. Perse's
fantastic longevity has safely tided symbolism far into
the twentieth century over the precarious storms
caused by other avant-garde movements which have in
the interim shaken the poets' serenity. He seems to
have illustrated in a multiplicity of facets the state of
mind that had made Valéry say at the end of "Le

Cimetière marin": "Il faut tenter de vivre!" In versification which effects a rendezvous between the prose poem and free verse, Perse has brought into reality the miracle of liberated verse, of which Baudelaire had dreamed in writing *Le Spleen de Paris*. No one is a greater master of this aspect of symbolism than St. John Perse. The abyss, which he most often identifies with the symbol of the "sea," and the life force, which is mirrored in the wind image, have so much flexibility that in general they avoid the fixed character of allegory.

Perse is a supreme technician, and ever more prolific and prodigious than Valéry in the virtuosity of his images. But he is also a more striking example of the mutations of symbolism—what I earlier called "denouement"—because he is somewhat removed from the "decadent" spirit. There is a vigor, a battling life spirit, which guards his landscapes from depopulation. With all the abstractions associated with physical sensation, there is a sense of a congested cosmos rather than of a desolate void in the symbolization of the universe. If Valéry is the last glow of the nineteenth-century light of symbolism, surviving as a brilliant fossil, as clear in its beauty as the rock which has become crystal, St. John Perse is the Apocryphal word. In that light, the symbolist orthodoxy of his poetry may be questioned, but the persistence in his work of the symbolist aura cannot be denied.

St. John Perse is not the only poet to shed the "decadent" spirit inherent in early symbolism, while retaining the verbal and metaphoric techniques of the symbolist movement. His Spanish contemporaries, such as Jorge Guillén and Jiménez, also inject this new mood into the symbolist vision: the correspondences of nature take on an invigorating character in their involvement with the human condition. The *mariposas* are gayer, the breeze sweeter. For instance, the image of the sea, in Jiménez as in Yeats, is linked with the voyage of the soul; but the "Nocturno soñado," the nocturnal dream, of which it is the apex is not an evasion of reality, but rather an acceptable counterpart, into which no brooding has permeated. We detect a return, full circle, to a more authentic Swedenborgian assurance of the correspondence of Heaven and earth:

La tierra lleva por la tierra;
mas tú, mar,
llevas por el cielo.
¡Con qué seguridad de luz de plata y oro,
nos marcan las estrellas
la ruta!—Se diría
que es la tierra el camino
del cuerpo,
que el mar es el camino
del alma—,
Sí, parece
que es el alma la sola viajera
del mar, que el cuerpo, solo,
se quedó allá en las playas,
sin ella, despidiéndola,
pesado, frío, igual que muerto.
¡Qué semejante
el viaje del mar al de la muerte,
al de la eterna vida!

The enumeration of these works taken out of their national contexts and traditions is not aimed at vain parallels, but to gauge through common traits and their individual variations, the wide range and orbit of the symbolist conventions and their survival beyond the Symbolist movement as a literary school. The failure or success attributed to this vein of modern poetry depends largely on the perspective of the viewer. If you look at the exaggerations of some of its conventions, at what the surrealist André Breton called "this universal swooning," it appears sterile. On the other hand, it looms as a gigantic and vital poetic force, which helped so many poets grow in their individual directions, opening up for them a great cosmic confrontation with reality. It allowed such writers as Eliot, Valéry, and Rilke to identify the poet as a seer, giving him an intellectual status that the poet had rarely enjoyed in his previous positions in the literary galaxy.

To the critical mind, and particularly when seen from the comparatist viewpoint, symbolism provides a fertile field for exploration, speculation, and discovery into what comprises one of the principal fountainheads of poetry, whose heritage has been shared on a broad international front. Indeed, seldom in the history of the arts has there been such a successful letting down of national frontiers, making the form of art which is most difficult to translate into a generously shared coin of spiritual exchange.

CONCLUSION

Is there a symbolist night after the sunset? Do any
of the styles and concepts associated with later movements—such as expressionism, dadaism, surrealism—
have a connection with symbolism? When Rimbaud
and Lautréamont are taken out of the symbolist galaxy, and Mallarmé is viewed as a precursor rather than
as a *chef d'école,* making him a more complex and
less doctrinaire writer, it becomes possible to contem-
plate surrealism, not as a movement that picked up
where symbolism left off, but as one that developed
concurrently, and merely reached its flowering somewhat later than symbolism. But what of dadaism? The
surrealists have led us to think that dadaism buried
itself in favor of surrealism around 1920, like a phoenix
ceding to new life; but we know now that that was a
fallacy. The truth of the matter is that dadaism did
not die; in many parts of the world it survives with
its ally, abstract art, to reinforce and cadence the persisting nihilism of the twentieth-century world.

While symbolism, like its predecessor, Romanticism,
becomes crystallized into a style that survives its doctrinaire phase, one can speculate about the extent to
which dadaism in literature, as well as in its so-called
avant-garde invasions of the drama and the cinema,
are offshoots of the symbolist outlook—with the addition of that soul-saving prop, black humor, which takes
self-consciousness away from the artist, and makes him
view his creation with the detachment of the universe

contemplating the human statement of its futility. The ephemeral and nihilistic subjects of symbolism were reduced to the "Rien," "Nothing," "Nada," of the dadaist cry. There was, however, a collectivity of negation in the dadaist movement, which was a strong deviation from the personal isolation of the symbolist poet. In terms of imagery, the dadaists accepted primarily metaphors suggestive of the void; but in their total disdain for human capacities, they departed from the cult of the ego.

In the "Verlorenes Ich" of the expressionist German poet Gottfried Benn, the ego seems totally gone astray when he says:

Verlorenes Ich, zersprengt von Stratosphären,
Opfer des Ion

Lost I, disintegrated by the stratosphere,
victim of ion

and ends the poem with the eternal symbolist interrogation of man's destiny and direction, which remains answerless:

Woher, wohin—, nicht Nacht, nicht Morgen
kein Evoë, kein Requiem,
du möchtest dir ein Stichwort borgen—,
allein bei wem?

Where? Whence? not night, not morning;
no Evoe, no requiem;
what you want is a borrowed formula—
only, from whom?

If the contemplation of self provides no solace because one is no longer even sure what or where the self is, the cult of language, which was such a boon for the symbolists, no longer offers any comfort, or any power to assuage the desolation of the human spirit.

In the theater, the non-sequential dialogue has been preserved—the bare stage; the lost and vagrant souls adrift in non-situated space, waiting for heaven knows what; and the correspondences with ludicrous beasts and barren trees, and insipid domestic objects. The emblems are more homey, the identification easier, because it is on a more pedestrian level.

In the cinema, the disconnected images produced by a Bergman or a Fellini are often the marks of purposeless living and inconclusive actions: bare hillsides; the purposeless rushing of trains; isolated beings, unseeing in their relationship to each other as they form an unrelated crowd. They no longer need masks because their faces *are* masks. Are the long corridors, the ancient statues of the ornate palace, the heroine of hazy origin and uncertain destination in *Last Year at Marienbad* anything more than a tired prolongation of the *Palais nomades* and the anemic princesses of the symbolists?

But if the silences and the drifting of characters suggest an even more acute rejection of reality than in nineteenth-century symbolism, the look of emptiness on a face can smack of the hollow as well as of the profound; if it is often indicative of transcendence of reality and of contact with a superior sphere, it can also be symptomatic of non-thinking and plain vegetation. In the most recent manifestations of the "decadent" spirit, it is hard to determine whether the look is of a bottomless pool, or the reflection from the foil of a mirror, creating an empty illusion. The eternal waiting of Estragon in Beckett's play *Waiting for Godot* outwardly assumes the same posture as that of the symbolist hero in the throes of delicate relationships with the universe. But there the comparison ends.

If it is uncertain whether the traits of the symbolist "decadent" can be observed in such prototypes, the power of cinematic art to create ambiguities of imagery is so far-reaching that it could easily perpetuate the symbolist technique in all the pictorial glory of its theory of correspondences and synesthesia, and give powerful dimensions to the ability to die in style! But the literary affiliations of the twentieth century have not yet been firmly classified. We have been more apt to group writers according to their "thought" than according to their style. For the present, the notion of avant-garde is as heterogeneous—including as it does the prevalence of both the symbolist and the surrealist vein—as it was in the early years of the Symbolist era.

AFTERWORD

In terms of literary history, Symbolism and Decadence are generally considered to have a dichoto-
mous relationship to each other. It is assumed that
they coexisted in the last two decades of the
nineteenth century, the former relating primarily to
poetry, the latter to prose. Symbolism was presumably concerned with aesthetics, and Decadence
reflected the deterioration of a system of ethics.

The avatars of Symbolism prevailed into the early
decades of the twentieth century, creating a beautiful
twilight poetry better defined as Mallarmean than
post-Symbolist. Viewing it as part of a Decadence
which indeed did not end with the end of the century,
helps to recognize a cohesion among some of the
greatest poets of our age who, otherwise, are left
dangling and in limbo in the annals of literary history
while primary attention is captured by the avant-
gardes of the new century. Paradoxically, the
apotheosis of a previous literary movement is often
overshadowed by the emergence of new ones.

Decadence means deterioration, but by relating to a
literary Byzantium, self-aware poets sensed that other
characteristic of the Decadent—what Mallarmé called
"la faute idéale de rose"—the rose fatality (so well
understood by Rilke)—supreme flowering of beauty
just before its demise.

The supersensitivity which in his last years led Mallarmé to orphic visions of the disintegration of self into speech—song in the broader sense of poetic discourse—was to continue uninterruptedly into the first quarter of the twentieth century as the major element of the *écriture* of the foremost poets of that era, principally of Valéry, Yeats, Rilke, Stevens. The number of major poetic works that came into print between 1919 and 1923 attest to this apogee of Mallarmé's heritage. These poets and their satellites do not form a literary movement in the accepted sense, and they are too important to be identified as post-symbolist or post anything. Their work constitutes a spectacular sunset; but in qualifying them as crepuscular it would not be proper to refer to a *waning* but to a terminal glow, extending hues into a global orbit. Rimbaud considered the color violet as the supreme radiance, the omega of his color alphabet. It is interesting to note that the violet ray, the ultimate and mysterious color of our earthly spectrum, penetrates this twilight poetry for which there is no other label than to call it the poetry of the decadence. An entire study could be done on the image of the violet ray in the poetry of the four poets I have designated here and of those for whom they served as models.

This decadence has no special connection with prose works generally associated with the label although paradoxically the poetry of the decadence may best be characterized as fiction. It is "fiction" in the sense in which Mallarmé used the word and to which Stevens gave its full significance in his ars poetica, *Toward a Supreme Fiction.* [1]

What Mallarmé was thinking when he labeled poetry "un art consacré aux fictions" in *Variations sur un sujet* [2] was the final rupture he conceived between

---

1 Michel Bénamou shows the direct relationship of the use of the word "fiction" in the two poets in his brilliant book, *L'Oeuvre-Monde de Wallace Stevens.*

2 Pléiade edition of his works, p. 368.

the real world and the poetic ontology of his inner being. When his atheistic rejection of the transcendental world left him with the meager gleanings of fields too amply harvested before him, he conjured the flower absent from all bouquets, and in the spirit of that essential but non-existent flora he struggled between nature and artifice, and finally he cloistered a fictitious universe having generic contiguity with the common ground of our perceptions. Yet the linguistic filter of the poet endows these images with the ultimate privacy and preservability. "Prose pour Des Esseintes" is indeed a subtle correction of Huysmans' misconception of what Mallarmé's private world really was:

D'ouïr tout le ciel et la carte
Sans fin attestés sur mes pas,
Par le flot même qui s'écarte
Que ce pays n'exista pas.

More poets of the fin de siècle took as their model the concept of Huysmans than of Mallarmé; Valéry was more subtle when in his original title he called *La Jeune Parque* "Iles," reminiscent of two other lines of *Prose*:

Oui, dans une île que l'air change
De vue et non de visions

This is certainly the significance of Yeats' vision of Byzantium as well; indeed the world of the poet of the decadence consists of islands, off the shores of our shared reality.

The fictional world of the poet does not merely construct absences; more often it explores worlds of the in-between, what Rilke called "Zwischenräume der Zeit" (*Sonnets to Orpheus*, Part II, no. 3); the mixed metaphor succeeds in referring at the same time to space and time. The sites of the in-between are the

loci of the poem; all the rest, what is called reality, is
so aptly described in Wallace Stevens' *The Man with the*
Blue Guitar:

Poetry is the subject of the poem
From this the poem issues and

To this returns. Between the two
Between issue and return, there is

An absence in reality
Things as they are, or so we say

Among the worlds of the in-between is the reflection
of Narcissus, which is neither Narcissus nor the water
but what Valéry called: "Cette tremblante, frêle et
pieuse distance/Entre moi-même et l'onde." [3] The vision of Orpheus is also of the in-between, neither of
this world nor of the underworld, but of nature
tinted with the memory of the other, visited for a
brief moment; it is the space in the mirror as Rilke
tells us in the Sonnets to Orpheus:

Spiegel: noch nie hat man wissend beschrieben,
was ihr in euerem Wesen seid.

the forbidden, inexpressible space through which
only the bold can pass such as the glowing Narcissus
(II, 3).

The in-between world contains objects of artifice
such as the golden bird of Yeats' Byzantium, which
represents the poet's triumph over nature. If indeed
he cancelled the overt line: "I fly from nature to
Byzantium," he did leave the vision of a world created
to overcome the decay and perishable character of
the natural world in his dream of the fake city that is
as much a reflection of his sense of being as the
shadow of Narcissus in the water is for Valéry. "And

3 "Fragments du Narcisse," Pléiade edition, Vol. I, p. 130.

gather me/Into the artifice of eternity," says Yeats. The same can be said of "The golden-feathered bird" in *L'Esthétique du mal* of Wallace Stevens. It is part of that "supreme fiction," the invented work, its meaning self-contained, independent of exterior forces, the triumph of man over gods, the creation of the violet space.

In the in-between world there emerges the shadowing presence of a figure, first perceived by Rimbaud as the radiant Génie; it is a Druid in Yeats, Figur or Angel in Rilke (assenting angel in the 10th Elegy), the necessary angel of earth in Stevens and sometimes the ephebe; and what else was "la Jeune Parque" in Valéry? Whereas the function of the standard angel in poetry is to make the invisible, the transcendental world *visible,* the angel of the poets of the decadence, who believe in no transcendental creatures, is to make the visible a little harder to see, as Stevens tells us, and in the ninth Elegy Rilke's angel asks whether it is not his dream to be invisible? The angel becomes in fact in this later poetry the human counterpoint of the absent flower of Mallarmé, more perfect than any to be plucked from our human contacts, non-existent yet recognizable. These alter egos of the poet provide a source of communication and a climate in the private world of the artist who can no longer talk with his fellowbeings nor breathe their standard air, nor tread the common soil. They are visible and invisible at the same time like the tree image which fascinates all these poets because it contains in its physical entity what has to be invented in the person of the angel. What is similar in the tree and the earth-angel? The tree is both visible and invisible like the imagined angel; its roots are not visible yet have to exist in order for the visible to prevail. It must also be capped by branches reaching out to another level of invisibility to give the sense of aspiration although the sense is known to be just an illusion, whereby the fiction of nature is paralleled and superseded by the fiction of the poet. In fact, in the seventeenth sonnet of Part II Rilke places the angels in the trees, fusing the parallel images into one. So the angel assumes a point of virtual contact with this world, though having an ontology of its own; it becomes a hyphen between the earthly and the conceivable but fictitious *elsewhere,* the concrete visualization of the abstract.

Finally, perhaps the most interesting aspect of the in-between is the perception of turning points: these turning points could be graded from the simplest to the most complicated. Mythical characters like Daphne and Hyacinth in Rilke and Stevens respectively are of the more obvious type. What is interesting in these transformations is not the fact of the transformation, but the passage from one to the other, the same kind of passage as from the visible to the invisible. More delicate is the probing of the turning point from consciousness to unconsciousness: this process is demonstrated in *La Jeune Parque* in the transition into and from sleep; of course the model for this pattern of passage was Mallarmé's *Igitur* where the in-between world was between life and death. As Valéry comments on the *passage* in *La Jeune Parque,* he observes:

Je me voyais me voir, sinueuse et dorais
De regards en regards, mes profondes forêts

If reference is made here to the correspondences of Baudelaire's "forêt de symboles," the forests are not exterior entities yielding knowledge of other worlds, but inner forests betraying knowledge of unconscious forces, the only area in which the poet can still seek mystery and revelation. The threshold of the unconscious is also the element of another kind of passage, the movement from the I to the All as Valéry explains in *L'Ame et la Danse:*

Cet *un* veut jouer à Tout
Il veut jouer à l'Universalité de l'Ame
Il veut remédier à son identité par le nombre de ses actes

Of course in the in-between world of Mallarmé's
Igitur the passage came dangerously close to mortal
oblivion, beyond both the I and the All. It is on the
edge of this Igitur world that Rilke hovers in his Sonnets. It is interesting to note that the myth of Orpheus
is utilized here not to suggest the pathos of a loss of a
loved one, but of the adjustments Orpheus has to
make in his meanderings in and out of the death
zone, and of the desire to permute one vision through
the other. The superpositions are very poignant in
sonnets 9, 16, and 26 in Part I. He says in no. 9:

Erst in dem Doppelbereich
werden die Stimmen
ewig und mild

The worlds of the in-between suggest a compromise between an unbelievable immortality and an
inacceptable mortality. These zones are, as we have
seen, both temporal and spacial.

But supersensitivity does not by itself constitute
poetry; it is only when the need for expression is
equal to the power to create that great poetry is
achieved. When the Symbolists communicated their
sense of the evanescent, of the ineffable, by using
nature as a mediator between their tangible percep-
tivity and its invisible target, they created a system of
metaphors suggestive of the abstract in terms of the
concrete; although they intentionally created verbal
ambiguities to enlarge the field of connotations, the
central medium of communication remained an-
chored in language. Their courtship of music, recognized as a salient quality of symbolist poetry, was an
effort to simulate the musical structure and the ap-

proximate musical sound with the phonemes of speech.

But the worlds of the in-between make greater demands on the poet's power over language until indeed it proves no longer adequate. Of course one way to overcome th inadequacy of language is silence. We know the poetic aphasia practiced by Mallarmé in *Un Coup de dés;* we know the intermittent silences of Maeterlinck and those of Beckett, and those of a great many dramatic writers in Spanish and Italian such as Lorca and Betti. But when Rilke longs to find a site where "spräche wäre, ohne sie spricht," in sonnet 20 part II, he is not talking about the communication of silences. He is thinking of the poet's appropriation of other media, not in terms of a simple simulation, but of the grasp of the power of expression as it may be appropriated from another medium for the verbal representations of the worlds of the in-between.

Some of these forms of communication suggested by these poets are the dance, music, sculpture, painting, equestrian skills; but this does not mean that the poet dances, sings, chisels his images, paints in words, rides his horse. He does not simulate in words their power of communication but uses them as a referential system when the need to express is not satisfied with the words at his command.

Interest in the dance was of course so evident in Mallarmé that when in his turn Valéry came to it he thought there was not much to add to what Mallarmé had already said: "Mallarmé avait épuisé le sujet en tant qu'il appartient à la littérature." (Pléiade, II, 1407) For Mallarmé the dancer was the supreme metaphor, it was a "poème dégagé de tout appareil de scribe"; [4] yet it was a language, a compact language, what he calls in *Crayonné au Théâtre* "prodige de raccourci." Valéry, Yeats, and Rilke had much to add to

[4] *Oeuvres*, p. 304.

Mallarmé's definition of the dance. For Valéry the dance is a poem, but it is also an act which instead of provoking movement creates *a state,* affecting the nature of things in a way that according to Valéry is more powerful than the impact of a philosophy or of a powerful dream.[5] In gestures he recognizes a series of turning points, making of the dance a locus of metamorphoses. What does all this mean in terms of the poetic process? The poet is not in the position of receiving the visual pleasure of the graceful dancer but of being the dancer and like the dancer acting upon the objective world, modifying it at will, creating a stance, communicating it to the reader by using words in the way in which the dancer cuts through obstacles of ether and substance. The dance suggests the transient character of life through movement in no. 18, part II of Rilke's sonnets. If these sonnets were in memory of the dancer, Vera, who had died prematurely, Rilke's poems in her honor are not eulogies, nor elegies. She becomes for him the power of welding the subject (i.e. the I) with the object (i.e. the dance) so that she merges with the greater identity even as she loses her personal one. It is particularly well expressed in Part I, no. 25 where the dancer is indeed the flower absent from all bouquets: "Wie eine Blume, vonder der ich den Namen nicht Weiss," he muses as she dances through the devouring open gate.

The other unspoken communication is music. Music's seduction of the Symbolists reaches a new phase in the poetry of Rilke and of Stevens. In both cases it is a unifying force in the universe. It is the second function of Orphism; if the first was to suggest an in-between world after his return from Hades, the second is to overcome the dismemberment which was inflicted on him in the myth. Instead of being the

5 Cf. *L'Ame et la Danse, Oeuvres,* Vol. II, p. 174.

symbol of disintegration, Orpheus becomes the agent
of unification. Part I, no. 26 begins and ends with
Orpheus' power of song but also of his power of endowing mortals with hearing. In Part II, no. 10 he
endows even the stone with hearing, although the
things that are heard are mostly "unsägliche." Music
alone can communicate in a believable way the sense
of the transcendent which the poets of whom we are
speaking can no longer accept intellectually. "Gesang
ist Dasein," says Rilke in Part I, no. 3, in rhythm is the
"unsichbares Gedicht" (Part II, no. 1).

In the case of Wallace Stevens music is the catalyst
of metamorphoses. The man with the Blue Guitar is
indeed Orpheus in a new guise: "Things as they
are/Are changed by the blue guitar."

These descendants of Mallarmé's orphism revital-
ize symbolism when it has already passed its meridian.
Although they rescue beauty for a while longer from
the forces tending toward its destruction, yet they be-
long in the context of decadence [6] because the glor-
ification of the evanescent does not alter its precarious condition. The temples and palaces of Byzantium
survived its sovereignty, but survival presumes an-
nihilation: the swan's last song, beautiful but unvi-
able, and unrepeatable. Those who tried to repeat the
anguish of Rilke, the yearning of Yeats, or the sober
stoicism of Valéry were anachronistic in their *écriture*
as in their epistemè. Sunsets, no matter how exquisite,
possess *la faute idéale de rose*. They fade into darkness,
and leave space for new dawns. The supreme fiction,
like all works of fiction, is precipitated toward a dé-
nouement. The poetic fiction, in spite of its glorious
apparition, was headed for dissolution. Between two
worlds both rejectable, the poet was caught in an im-

[6] Stevens survived himself to a certain degree by overcoming the
forces of decadence in effecting a successful transplant of the fiction of the poet upon a prime reality. Perhaps Ameria was the
differential factor.

passe and created a poetry of unease, of alienation. It had the forces of its impotence, irreconcilable, vulnerable. It contained a mechanism for self-annihilation. It evolved into what Anais Nin has magnificently called "The Winter of Artifice."

The poet had to find new ways to cope with reality, to make his peace with nature, find new sources of beauty in harmony with a new apprehension of the forces of the natural universe. The chthonian experiences of modern poets such as André Breton, Octavio Paz, Leopold Senghor, are those of Orpheuses who can breathe longer underground, can conceive poetry within the dimensions of the natural instead of an artificial world. Their interest in metamorphosis relates to totality and to the unity of existence rather than to such delicate, imperceptible discernments as the turning points expressed in the avatars of symbolism. The between-worlds disappear as the inward probing of the new poets makes this world without any illusions more acceptable than in its dichotomies. Had not Valéry sensed the changing winds without really being capable of participating in the new departures, when in "Le Cimetière marin" he said "Le vent se lève, il faut tenter de vivre"?

But if the wind changed and some sailed off toward new horizons, it did not disperse the stockpile of poetic leaves, it did not destroy that immense power to fertilize, which was inherent in symbolism.

June 15, 1977
Old Westbury

BIBLIOGRAPHY

This is a working bibliography as of 1966; a much more complete and international bibliography is now available in David L. Anderson, *Symbolism: A Bibliography of Symbolism as an International and Multi-Disciplinary Movement*, New York, New York University Press, 1975. See also Krawitz, Henry, A post-symbolist bibliography. Scarecrow Press, N.J., 1973.

AUSTIN, LLOYD JAMES. "'L'Après-midi d'un faune'" *Studi in Onore di Carlo Pellegrini*, Biblioteca di "Studi Francesi," Torino, Vol. II, 1963.
————. *L'Univers poétique de Baudelaire: Symbolisme et Symbolique*, Paris, Mercure de France, 1956.
BALAKIAN, ANNA. "Studies in French Symbolism, 1945–1955," *The Romanic Review*, XLVI, No. 3, October 1955, 223–30.
BALDENSPERGER, FERNAND. *Orientations étrangères chez Honoré de Balzac*, Paris, Champion, 1927.
BARRE, ANDRÉ. *Le Symbolisme*, Paris, Jouve, 1911.
BASTIDE, ROGER. *A Poesia Afro-Brasileira*, São Paulo, Livraria Martins, 1943.
BÉGUIN, ALBERT. *L'Ame romantique et le Rêve* (1937), 2 volumes, Paris, Corti, 1946 (new edition).
BENNETT, EDWIN KEPPEL. *Stefan George*, Cambridge, Bowes & Bowes, 1954.
BENRATH, HENRY. *Stefan George*, Paris, Librairie Stock, 1936.
BERNARDINI, ADA P. *Simbolisti e decadenti*, Rome, 1935.
BERTOCCI, ANGELO P. *From Symbolism to Baudelaire*, Carbondale, Southern Illinois University Press, 1964.
BINNI, WALTER. *La Poetica del decadentismo*, Florence, G. C. Sansoni, 1936.
BLOCK, HASKELL. *Mallarmé and the Symbolist Drama*, Detroit, Wayne State University Press, 1963.
BOWRA, C. M. *The Creative Experiment*, London, Macmillan, 1949.
————. *The Heritage of Symbolism*, London, Macmillan, 1943.
CAZAMIAN, LOUIS. *Symbolisme et poésie*, Neuchâtel, Editions de la Baconnière, 1947.
CHARPENTIER, JOHN. *Le Symbolisme*, Paris, Les Arts et le Livre, 1927.
CHASSÉ, CHARLES. *Les Clefs de Mallarmé*, Paris, Aubier, Editions Montaigne, 1954.
CHIARI, JOSEPH. *Symbolism from Poe to Mallarmé*, London Rockliff, 1956.

CORNELL, KENNETH. *The Symbolist Movement*, New Haven, Yale University Press, 1951.

————. *The Post-Symbolist Period*. New Haven, Yale University Press, 1958.

CRAIG, G. DUNDAS. *The Modernist Trend in Spanish American Poetry*, Berkeley, University of California Press, 1934. (Anthology in original with literal translations in English and critical introduction and commentary on each poet.)

DÉCAUDIN, MICHEL. *La crise des valeurs symbolistes: vingt ans de poésie française, 1895–1914*, Toulouse, Privat, 1960.

DELFEL, GUY. *L'Esthétique de Stéphane Mallarmé*, Paris, Flammarion, 1951.

DOISY, MARCEL. *Paul Valéry: Intelligence et poésie*, Paris Cercle du Livre, 1952.

DONCHIN, GEORGETTE. *The Influence of French Symbolism on Russian Poetry*, Gravenhage, Mouton & Company, 1958.

DUTHIE, ENID L. *L'Influence du symbolisme français dans le renouveau poétique de l'Allemagne: les Blätter für die Kunst de 1892 à 1900*, Paris, Champion, 1933.

ELIOT, T. S. *Selected Essays*, New York, Harcourt, Brace & Company, 1932.

————. *The Sacred Wood*, London, Methuen & Company, 1928 (2nd edition).

FEIDELSON, CHARLES. *Symbolism and American Literature*, Chicago, University of Chicago Press, 1953.

FLORA, FRANCESCO. *La poesia ermetica*, Bari, G. Laterza, 1936.

FRIEDRICH, HUGO. *Die Struktur der modernen Lyrik von Baudelaire bis zur Gegenwart*, Hamburg, Rowohlt, 1960.

GENGOUX, JACQUES. *Le Symbolisme de Mallarmé*, Paris, Nizet, 1950.

GEORGE, STEFAN. *The Works of Stefan George*, translated by Olga Marx and Ernst Morwitz, Chapel Hill, North Carolina University Press, 1949.

————. *Blätter für die Kunst*, Berlin, Carl August Klein, 1892–1919.

————. *Poems*, translated by Carol North Valhope and Ernst Morwitz, New York, Pantheon Books, 1943. (Bilingual edition.)

GHIL, RENÉ. *Les dates et les oeuvres: symbolisme et poésie scientifique*, Paris, G. Crès, 1923.

GOSSE, EDMUND. *Leaves and Fruit*, London, W. Heinemann, 1927.

GOURMONT, RÉMY DE. *Promenades littéraires*, Paris, Mercure de France, 1904.

GREENE, E. J. H. "Jules Laforgue et T. S. Eliot," *Revue de Littérature comparée*, Paris, July-September 1948, pp. 363–97.

GRIFFIN, WILLIAM J. "Brazilian Literature in English Translation," *Revista interamericana de bibliografía*, Washington, D.C., Pan American Union, Vol. 5, Nos. 1–2, 1955.

GUICHARD, LÉON. *Jules Laforgue et ses poésies*, Paris, Presses Universitaires de France, 1950.

GUIRAUD, PIERRE. *Index du vocabulaire du symbolisme*, Paris, Klincksieck, 1953.

HAMBURGER, MICHAEL. *Reason and Energy; Studies in German Literature*, New York, Grove Press, 1957.

HOFMANNSTHAL, HUGO VON. *Poems and Verse Plays*, edited and introduced by Michael Hamburger, with a preface by T. S. Eliot, New York, Pantheon Books, 1961. (Bilingual edition.)

HURET, JULES. *Enquête sur l'Evolution littéraire*, Paris, Charpentier, 1891.

HYTIER, JEAN. *La Poétique de Valéry*, Paris, Colin, 1953.

JASPER, GERTRUDE. *Adventures into Theater: Lugné-Poe and the Théâtre de l'Oeuvre to 1889*, New Brunswick, Rutgers University Press, 1947.

JOHANSEN, SVEN. *Le Symbolisme*, Copenhagen, Einar Munksgaard, 1945.

JONES, P. MANSELL. *The Background of Modern French Poetry*, Cambridge, Cambridge University Press, 1951.

KAHN, GUSTAVE. *Les origines du symbolisme*, Paris, A. Messein, 1936.

————. *Symbolistes et Décadents*, Paris, Vanier, 1902.

LEHMANN, ANDREW GEORGE. *The Symbolist Aesthetic in France, 1885–1895*, Oxford, Basin Blackwell, 1950.

LETHÈVE, JACQUES. *Impressionnistes et symbolistes devant la presse*, Paris, A. Colin, 1959.

LEVIN, HARRY. *The Power of Blackness: Hawthorne, Poe, Melville*, New York, Knopf, 1958.

MacINTYRE, C. F. *French Symbolist Poetry*, Berkeley, University of California Press, 1958.

————. *Fifty Selected Poems* (Translations from Rilke), Berkeley, University of California Press, 1940.

MARITAIN, JACQUES. *Frontières de la Poésie*, Paris, Louis Rouart et fils, 1935. Translated by Joseph W. Evans under the title *Art and Scholasticism, and the Frontiers of Poetry*, New York, Scribner, 1962.

MASLENIKOV, OLEG A. *The Frenzied Poets: Audrey Biely and the Russian Symbolists*, Berkeley, University of California Press, 1952.

MATHEWS, JACKSON. *La Wallonie 1886–1892*, New York, King's Crown Press, 1947.

MARTINO, PIERRE. *Parnasse et Symbolisme*, Paris, Colin, 1923.

MICHAUD, GUY. *Mallarmé: l'homme et l'oeuvre*, Paris, Hatier-Boivin, 1953.

————. *Message poétique du symbolisme*, Paris, Nizet, 1947.

————. *La doctrine symboliste*, documents, Paris, Nizet, 1947.

MOORE, GEORGE. *Confessions of a Young Man*, New York, Brentano Editions, 1920.

————. *Memoirs of My Dead Life*, London, W. Heinemann, 1923.

MOREAU, PIERRE. "Symbole, Symbolique, Symbolisme," *CAIEF*, No. 6, 1954.

MORICE, C. *La littérature de tout à l'heure*, Paris, Perrin, 1889.

MURICY, ANDRADE. *Panorama do movimento simbolista brasileiro*, 3 vols., Rio de Janeiro, Departamento de Imprensa Nacional, 1951–1952. (Selections of prose and poetry of over 105 writers considered symbolist.)

NEAPES, ERWIN KEMPTON. *L'Influence française dans l'oeuvre de Rubén Dario*, Paris, Champion, 1921.

NORDAU, MAX. *Degeneration*, translated from German, New York, Appleton, 1912 (4th edition).

NOULET, E. *Stéphane Mallarmé*, Paris, E. Droz, 1940.

The Oxford Book of Portuguese Verse, Oxford, Clarendon Press, 1921.

PICA, VITTORIO. *Letterature d'eccezione*, Milan, Baldini-Castoldi, 1899.

PICCO, F. "Simbolismo francese e simbolismo italiano," *Nuova Antologia*, Rome, May 1, 1926, pp. 82–91.

POMMIER, JEAN. *La Mystique de Baudelaire*, Paris, Belles Lettres, 1932.

PUTNAM, SAMUEL. *Marvelous Journey: A survey of four centuries of Brazilian writing*, New York, Knopf, 1948.

QUASIMODO, SALVATORE. *Discourse on Poetry*, translated by A. Mandelbaum, New York, Noonday Press, 1961.

————. *Selected Writings of Salvatore Quasimodo*, 100 poems, edited and translated by A. Mandelbaum, New York, Farrar, Straus & Cudahy, 1960.

QUENNELL, PETER. *Baudelaire and the Symbolists*, London, Weidenfeld and Nicolson, 1954.

RAGUSA, OLGA. "French Symbolism in Italy," *The Romanic Review*, Vol. XLVI, No. 3, October 1955, pp. 231–35.

————. *Mallarmé in Italy: Literary Influence and Critical Response*, New York, S. F. Vanni, 1957.

RAMSEY, WARREN. *Jules Laforgue and the Ironic Inheritance*, New York, Oxford University Press, 1953.

RAYMOND, MARCEL. *De Baudelaire au surréalisme*, Paris, Corréa, 1933.

RICHARD, NOËL. *A l'aube du symbolisme*, Paris, Nizet, 1961.

Romanic Review, Vol. XLVI, No. 3, October 1955 (entire issue devoted to French Symbolism).

ROMANO, SALVATORE. *Poetica dell'ermetismo,* Florence, 1942.

SCARFE, FRANCIS. *The Art of Paul Valéry,* London, W. Heinemann, 1954.

SCHÉRER, JACQUES. *L'Expression littéraire dans l'oeuvre de Mallarmé,* Paris, Droz, 1947.

SEWELL, ELIZABETH. *Paul Valéry: The Mind in the Mirror,* New Haven, Yale University Press, 1952.

STAHL, E. L. "The Genesis of Symbolist Theories in Germany," *Modern Language Review,* 41 (1946), 306–17.

STARKIE, ENID. *Baudelaire,* New York, G. P. Putnam, 1933.

SUCKLING, NORMAN. *Paul Valéry and the Civilized Mind,* New York, Oxford Press, 1954.

SUGAR, L. DE. *Baudelaire et R. M. Rilke,* Paris, Nouvelles Editions Latines, 1954.

SYMONS, ARTHUR. *The Symbolist Movement in Literature,* London, Constable, 1899; New York, Dutton, 1958.

TASSO DE SILVEIRA. "A Poesia simbolista em Portugal," *Ocidente,* Lisbon, Vol. 26, July 1945, pp. 150–58.

TAUPIN, RENÉ. *L'Influence du symbolisme français sur la poésie américaine de 1910 à 1920,* Paris, Champion, 1929.

TEMPLE, RUTH Z. *The Critic's Alchemy, A Study of the Introduction of French Symbolism into England,* New York, Twayne, 1953.

TINDALL, W. Y. *The Literary Symbol,* New York, Columbia University Press, 1955.

VIATTE, AUGUSTE. *Victor Hugo et les Illuminés de son temps,* Montreal, Editions de l'Arbre, 1942.

WEEVERS, THEODOOR. *Poetry of the Netherlands in Its European Context, 1170–1930,* Illustrated with poem in original and in translation, London, University of London, The Athlone Press, 1960.

WELLEK, RENÉ. *A History of Modern Criticism, 1750–1950,* Vol. 2, *The Romantic Age,* New Haven, Yale University Press, 1955.

WILSON, EDMUND. *Axel's Castle,* New York, Scribner, 1936.

YARMOLINSKY, AVRAHM, ed. *An Anthology of Russian Verse,* New York, Anchor Books, 1962.

YEATS, W. B. "The Symbolism of Poetry" and "Louis Lambert," *Essays and Introductions,* New York, Macmillan, 1961.

———. "The Trembling of the Veil," *Autobiographies,* London, Macmillan, 1926.

INDEX